SELL YOUR HOME IN CANADA

Geraldine Santiago

Self-Counsel Press
(a division of)
International Self-Counsel Press Ltd.
Canada   USA

Self-Counsel Press acknowledges the financial support of the Government of Canada through the Book Publishing Industry Development Program (BPIDP) for our publishing activities.

Printed in Canada

First edition: 2005

Library and Archives Canada Cataloguing in Publication

Santiago, Geraldine
    Sell your home in Canada / Geraldine Santiago.

(Self-counsel reference series)
ISBN 1-55180-599-5

1. House selling—Canada. I. Title. II. Series.
HD1379.S266 2005   643'.12'0971   C2004-906766-4

Permissions Acknowledgements

Sample 3: Inspection Summary by Glenn Duxbury & Associates Building Inspection and Consulting is used with permission.

Sample 4: Summary Appraisal Report by Macintosh Appraisal Ltd. is used with permission.

The text on page 56 discussing the most difficult tasks for FSBOS, reprinted from "The 2004 National Association of REALTORS® Profile of Home Buyers and Sellers," ©2004 National Association of REALTORS®, is used with permission.

Self-Counsel Press
(a division of)
International Self-Counsel Press Ltd.

1481 Charlotte Road	1704 North State Street
North Vancouver, BC V7J 1H1	Bellingham, WA 98225
Canada	USA

CONTENTS

INTRODUCTION   xi

PART 1: WHERE SHOULD I BEGIN?   1

1   WHAT TYPE OF MARKET IS IT?   3

Buyer's Market   3

Seller's Market   4

Balanced Market   4

When Is the Best Time to Sell?   4

2   WHO WILL BUY YOUR HOME?   5

3   KNOWING YOUR HOME IS THE KEY   7

Types of Homes   7

Title and Ownership   8

   Co-ownership   8

   Strata title   8

   Co-operative   9

   Timeshares   9

	Freehold	9
	Leasehold	9
	Positive and Negative Aspects of Your Property	10
	Selling the Neighbourhood and the Community	11
	Selling a Condo	11
	Selling a Rental Property	12
	Selling an Older Home	12

4 GATHERING DATA AND LEGAL DOCUMENTATION — 15

Title Search	16
Survey Certificate	17
New Home Warranty Information	17
Property Condition Disclosure Statement (PCDS)	19
Oil Tank Removal	22
Zoning Information	23
City Assessment	23
Other Information for Strata Property	24
Other Documentation	25
Measuring Your Property	25
Pre-Sale Building Inspection	27

5 SELLING YOUR HOME: WHAT IS IT WORTH? — 33

Why Are You Selling?	33
What Is Your Home Worth?	33
What is a comparative market analysis (CMA)?	34
Increasing or decreasing your price	39
Pricing land only	40
Renovation value	40
What If You Have a Mortgage?	41
Getting a new mortgage	41
Bridge loans	42
Portable mortgage	42
Vendor take-back mortgage	43
Assumable mortgage	43

PART 2: SHOULD I SELL MY OWN HOME OR GET HELP? 51

6   SELLING ON YOUR OWN OR WITH A REAL ESTATE AGENT 53

What Are the Costs of Selling a Property? 53

Do You Have What It Takes to Sell Your Own Home? 54

What Are the Pitfalls of Selling without an Agent? 55

What Are the Benefits of Going with an Agent? 57

    Should you get a full-service agent or do you want to be involved? 58

    Choosing the right agent for you 59

    What about a team of agents? 60

    Types of listings 60

    The listing agreement 61

    Responsibilities of listing agents 62

    Legal and professional requirements for agents 62

The Agent's Commission 65

    Full commission on a quick sale 66

    How can you save on commission? 66

    Bonuses and other incentives for agents 67

What Is the MLS System and What Can It Do for Sellers? 67

PART 3: HOW DO I GO FROM MARKETING TO COMPLETING THE SALE? 69

7   MARKETING YOUR HOME 71

What Do You Do to Market a Property? 71

    Print advertising and websites 72

    Signage and tools of the trade 73

    Marketing to friends, relatives, and neighbours 73

Advertising 74

8   SHOWING YOUR HOME 77

Protecting Yourself and Your Family 78

Showcasing Made Simple 78

Showing a Rental Property 80

Showing a Vacation Home 81

Open Houses and Agent Tours 81

9	**THE OFFER**	85
	The Buyer	86
	Separating qualified buyers from the lookers	86
	Who can be legally bound by a contract?	87
	When You Receive an Offer	87
	Condition precedents	87
	Time clauses	88
	Financing	88
	When You Receive Multiple Offers, Low-ball Offers, or Agent Offers	89
	Competing offers, multiple offers, and back-up offers	90
	Identical or nearly identical offers	90
	Low-ball offers	91
	Offers from salespeople to purchase for themselves	91
	Negotiating a Sale	92
	What to negotiate	93
	Selling your furniture	93
	When You Reach an Agreement	94
	Deposits and down payments	94
	What if the building does not pass inspection?	95
	Showing after accepting an offer	96
	When Condition Precedents Are Met	96
10	**CLOSING, COMPLETION, AND POSSESSION**	103
	The Closing Procedure	103
	What Happens at Completion?	104
	Completion must be done on a weekday	105
	Hiccups at completion	107
	Possession	107
	When do you hand over the keys?	107
	What should you leave behind on possession day?	108
	What should you not leave behind?	108
	Doing a walk-through with the buyer or buyer's agent	109
	A special touch	109

CONCLUSION   111

APPENDIX 1 — REAL ESTATE ASSOCIATIONS AND BOARDS   113

APPENDIX 2 — RESOURCE LIST FOR OIL TANK SAFETY   117

**APPENDIX 3 — PROVINCIAL MINISTRIES AND DEPARTMENTS
OF HOUSING**   121

**APPENDIX 4 — CANADIAN ASSOCIATIONS OF HOME AND
PROPERTY INSPECTORS**   125

GLOSSARY   127

CHECKLISTS

  1   Documents and Information   30

  2   The Contract   97

  3   Service Arrangements   110

SAMPLES

  1   Title Search   18

  2   Property Condition Disclosure Statement   20

  3   Inspection Summary   28

  4   Summary Appraisal Report   35

  5   Comparative Market Analysis   44

  6   Listing Agreement   63

  7   Agreement of Purchase and Sale   99

  8   Addendum   101

  9   Seller's Statement of Adjustments   106

TABLES

  1   Types of Buyers and How to Target Them   6

  2   Provincial Associations of Home and Property Inspectors   29

NOTICE TO READERS

ACKNOWLEDGEMENTS

I gratefully acknowledge the important contributions made by other people in writing this book.

Thank you to John Santos-Ocampo of Invis for his contributions with regard to mortgages and to Glenn Duxbury for his contributions regarding home inspections.

To my friend and colleague Theresa Lee, thank you for your support, your encouragement, and your input.

Thank you to Richard Day at Self-Counsel Press for giving me the opportunity to write this book. Thank you to the editors, Audrey McClellan and Tanya Howe, and to everyone at Self-Counsel Press.

I wish to also thank my parents, Danilo and Lina, for their continued guidance and support. Last but not least, thank you to my husband, David, and my two daughters, Luisa and Lauren, who are my inspiration.

INTRODUCTION

If you are thinking of selling your home, there are many things you need to do before a "For Sale" sign goes up. Whether you are planning to sell your home on your own or with an agent, it will take a lot of co-ordination, organization, and work. Part 1 of this book covers the first things you need to do:

- Determine what kind of market you will be selling in: Is it a buyer's or seller's market or is it balanced? (See Chapter 1.)

- Decide who your target market is: Is your house suitable for first-time buyers, empty nesters, investors, or other types of buyers? (See Chapter 2.)

- Know your product: Find out details about your home that buyers will want to know. (See Chapter 3.)

- Gather the paperwork you'll need for selling your home: This includes legal material such as a title search, financial material such as tax records and mortgage information, and by-laws and financial reports for a strata title property. (See Chapter 4.)

- Determine a fair market price for your property: You can do this yourself or have a real estate agent or appraiser help. (See Chapter 5.)

Part 2 helps you with the decision of whether you should sell your home yourself, or if you should engage a partial-service or full-service realty company. Part 2 discusses the following factors that will help you with your decision:

- Costs of selling your property
- Requirements for marketing your property
- Personality and ability needed to sell the property yourself
- Pitfalls of selling without a real estate agent
- Services offered by a real estate agent

Part 3 includes information on marketing and completion, covering the following important topics:

- Advertising
- Showing your property
- Understanding what to do when an offer is made
- Completing the sale

Selling your home can be an empowering experience, but it is important to understand how to do it properly to gain the best value for your home. Gaining knowledge about selling your home can help you make the right decisions and reduce the stress that may come with selling your home. Visit real estate websites, read books about selling a home, and attend seminars; get as much information as you can about the processes and costs of selling your home before you get into the real estate market.

This book is intended to help home sellers become familiar with the many processes involved in selling a home. I hope this book will give you confidence in your own choices and decisions and make your selling experience a pleasant one!

PART 1
WHERE SHOULD I BEGIN?

Chapter 1
WHAT TYPE OF MARKET IS IT?

Before you put your home up for sale, it is important to look at the larger market conditions, such as local and national housing prices, mortgage rate movements, and new home construction. The Canada Mortgage and Housing Corporation (CMHC) helps people selling their homes understand how the housing market is evolving. The CMHC's regional offices and Market Analysis Centre are great sources for finding out about the current housing market. The CMHC regularly publishes local market analysis reports and provides information on recent trends in housing market conditions across the country.

Your regional CMHC market analyst can tell you if it's a buyer's, seller's, or balanced housing market. Contact information for market analysts is available on the CMHC website at <www.cmhc-schl.gc.ca/en/contact/contacten_021.cfm>, or you can order the most popular housing reports online from the CMHC site <www.cmhc-schl.gc.ca/> and they will be e-mailed to you in PDF, Lotus, or Excel format.

Buyer's Market

In a buyer's market, the number of homes available for sale exceeds the demand, so prices will either stabilize or drop. With

fewer buyers and more homes, buyers have greater negotiating leverage, so sellers should price their homes competitively if they want to sell.

Seller's Market

In a seller's market, relatively few homes are on the market, so the number of buyers exceeds the number of sellers and the seller dictates the price. In this situation of low inventory, sellers often get their price (sometimes more than the asking price) because of a bidding war, in which there are many competing offers.

Balanced Market

In a balanced market, there is an equal number of buyers and sellers. If you are a seller in this market, you will probably not experience a bidding war because there are enough properties listed on the market.

When Is the Best Time to Sell?

The busiest times in the real estate industry are usually the spring and summer. This is when many companies relocate their employees, and as a result there are more properties to choose from. Because of this availability, many buyers tend to do their home shopping at this time, so there is the most competition among buyers. A recent poll showed that Canadians feel that April, May, and June are the best times to sell a home and December and January are the best times to buy a home.

If you are selling your home in order to move up to a new house, another major influence on deciding when to sell is the mortgage interest rate. What rates are available now? Will they fall or will they rise in the near future? If they rise, how much will they go up? It can be hard to answer these questions, but CMHC's Market Analysis Centre can help by providing you with both an analysis of the current mortgage market and an outlook for future mortgage rates.

Chapter 2
WHO WILL BUY YOUR HOME?

It is important, when selling any product, to determine who your target market is so that you can attract the right buyer. For example, if your home is ideal for first-time home-buyers, you would market it differently than you would if you were trying to attract empty nesters. If you were selling to first-time buyers, you would use key words and phrases such as "room to grow," "great den for your family," or "ample backyard space." Table 1 lists the types of buyers, what they might be looking for, and how to let them know about your property.

Knowing the demographic you are trying to attract will also help when you are deciding where to advertise your home. If a newspaper magazine is targeted to first-time home-buyers, for example, and you've got a great starter home, you may want to include an advertisement in that magazine. If you are selling an investment property, you would think about advertising in an investment-related trade magazine, using phrases such as "great for first-time investor" and "positive cash flow." For the empty nester market, "downsizing" or "less maintenance" may be appealing descriptions, and you might place an ad in seniors' magazines.

Table 1
TYPES OF BUYERS AND HOW TO TARGET THEM

Type of Buyer	Type of Home	Use Words Like	Advertise In
First-time buyers	Condo, bungalow	Room to grow	Community centre, library, classified ads
Young couples	Condo, townhouse, loft	Great space, den can be converted	Community centre, public library, classified ads
Young families	Townhouse, bungalow with in-law suite or basement suite	Front and backyard, tree-lined street, quiet neighbourhood	Community newspapers, public library, community centre
Move-up buyers	Townhouse, house	Recreation room, huge patio and deck	Community newspapers, public library, community centre
Do-it-yourselfers	Detached home	Needs TLC, upgrades required	Classified ads, building centre
Professionals	Condo, loft, studio space	Centrally located, gym, fitness centre, spa	Classified ads and professional magazines, fitness groups, coffee shops downtown
Investors	Condo, multi-family	Great revenue, revenue potential	Classified ads
Empty nesters	Condo, townhouse	Quiet, great amenities, close to shopping, patio/deck	Seniors' groups, community centre, seniors' newspapers, churches

Chapter 3

KNOWING YOUR HOME IS THE KEY

Knowing your product is the key to selling. Knowing information about your home will help you determine your target market, will allow you to answer buyers' questions, and will let you decide how to sell your home, including whether you use a real estate agent or sell it on your own. Some of the most important things you need to know are the type of home you are selling, the type of ownership you have and how that affects what you can sell, and the features of your home and neighbourhood.

Types of Homes

The type of home you have — whether detached, semi-detached (often called a duplex or townhouse), apartment, condominium, or manufactured home/mobile home — will determine the type of market you are selling to. For example, a single-family detached home will be ideal for a young couple, a young family, or a first-time home-buyer. Young couples or singles, as well as professionals and investors, will be attracted to a condominium or apartment.

A condominium is a type of housing ownership, more formally known as strata title ownership, rather than a particular type of housing. (There is more detail on strata title later in this chapter.)

Understanding the different types of home ownership is important.

Title and Ownership

When you are preparing to sell a property, you need to understand the different types of home ownership and how they appear on the land title. The most common types of residential home ownership are: co-ownership (including joint tenancy and tenancy in common), strata title, co-operative, timeshares (including fee ownership interest and right-to-use ownership), freehold, and leasehold.

Co-ownership

Co-ownership occurs if property is owned by more than one person. This type of ownership is generally either by joint tenancy or by tenancy in common. A notary or lawyer should be able to explain the differences between the two types of ownership and how the co-ownership in your situation affects your ability to sell the property. A notary or lawyer can also tell you how you should be registered on the title.

Joint tenancy

When you purchase with a spouse or partner, you commonly have *joint tenancy*. When one partner dies, the other becomes the sole owner. The ownership automatically transfers to the survivor without having to go through probate. This feature is known as the right of survivorship. A joint tenant cannot leave the property interest in a will to a third party. If you and your spouse divorce, or you and a partner have a falling out, you may not be able to sell a property held in joint tenancy. Depending on how you are listed on the title, you may need your spouse's or partner's consent to sell. A lawyer will be able to tell you what legal interest each of you owns and what other options are available to you.

Tenancy in common

Tenancy in common is a form of co-ownership that may involve two or more owners. Each owner may or may not have the same amount of shares, rights, or interests. As a result, one party may sell his or her share without the permission of others.

Strata title

In strata title, you not only own your unit, but also share ownership of the common areas of the strata property, such as hallways, garages, and elevators. Because you share these common areas, you share the financial responsibility for their maintenance with the other owners of the building. This will be reflected in your monthly maintenance fees.

Co-operative

A co-operative is a type of ownership in which the property is owned in the name of a company. Buyers purchase shares in the company, which gives them ownership of a suite and often of a parking stall as well. In a condominium or co-operative, you will be governed by the strata corporation or company's by-laws and regulations. You will be required to live under those rules and regulations and will be fined for violations. If you don't pay your fines, assessments, or monthly dues, the strata corporation or homeowners' association can put a lien on your home.

Timeshares

Timeshares are a relatively new concept in property ownership that generally fall under two main categories: fee ownership interest and right-to-use ownership. In fee ownership interest, the owner has a right to encumber, convey, or otherwise transfer the interest for all future time. In a right-to-use ownership, the buyer receives no registerable title. Instead, the owner of this interest has a contractual right to enjoy the use of the property for a specific period.

Many provinces do not currently have legislation specifically addressing timeshare ownership. If you have this type of property, seek the advice of a lawyer or your local real estate agent.

Freehold

A freehold interest is the same as "ownership" of property. The owner of a freehold interest has full use and control of the land and the buildings on it, subject to the rights of the Crown, local land-use by-laws, and other restrictions in place at the time of purchase.

Leasehold

A leasehold interest in land means the townhouse, apartment, or detached home is built on city-owned land. The term "leasehold" can also apply to single detached houses on farm land, on First

Nations land, and so on. Leasehold interests are for a defined period of time. They can be for a week, a month, a year, 99 years, or any other specific period of time. The person to whom leasehold interest is granted is called a lessee or tenant, and the grantor of the interest is called the lessor or the landlord. If a leasehold has a fixed term of 99 years, for example, there will be no review of the lease rate for the full 99 years. If the previous lessee has lived in a building on the leasehold for 20 years, you may purchase the remaining portion of 79 years. The shorter the remaining portion, the less a buyer will pay for the leasehold interest.

It is important to know that the sale of a leasehold differs greatly from the sale of a freehold property. For one thing, pricing does not reflect market value; you are only selling the improvements on the land, and not the land itself. If you are selling a leasehold property, financing may be a buyer's biggest obstacle, as many institutions will not finance this type of sale. To help buyers, you should try to provide a list of financial institutions that are receptive to financing this type of sale.

Further, many institutions may want a larger down payment to protect themselves from buyers who simply walk away from the property should there be a problem down the road. Other financial institutions may want to make sure that the prepaid lease has a long lifespan, 99 years or more.

Positive and Negative Aspects of Your Property

When you prepare to sell your home, you need to make a list of all the positive and negative aspects of your property. Some of the positive aspects may be distance to school, access to transportation, distance to the city centre, and distance to parks and community centre facilities. Though it is tempting to exaggerate the positive features of your property, it is dangerous to provide anything other than an accurate representation in all advertising and promotional material, or during showings to potential buyers. If you misrepresent the property you are selling, the buyer could sue you.

All homes have at least one negative aspect. Some negative aspects include an irregularly shaped lot or its location (e.g., Is your home on a busy main road? Is it too close to the golf course or train tracks?).

Highlight the positive aspects of your home as much as possible. Buyers will probably notice the negative aspects themselves.

Also remember that some negative aspects may not be entirely negative to some people. For instance, having a golf course nearby may be ideal for seniors, or being on a main road may be great for someone who doesn't drive.

Selling the Neighbourhood and the Community

When you purchased your home, you were probably also sold on the neighbourhood and broader community. These are great selling features that you should emphasize for potential buyers. For example, you may want to tell them about nearby schools, recreation centres providing year-round activities for the community, parks, hospitals, shopping centres, and places of worship. If you are selling your home to a young couple or young family, indicate how close they are to the nearest elementary school or daycare centre.

Make sure you let all potential buyers know what services are provided by the city, such as police, ambulance, garbage collection, mail delivery, fire protection, or snow removal. Buyers will also want to know about accessibility to your neighbourhood — is public transportation frequent and reliable, is there easy access to express routes, and so on.

Selling a Condo

If your home is a strata type of ownership, find out some of the basic information that buyers always ask about this kind of property, such as the amount in the contingency fund; what repairs (if any) have been done or will be done in the future; what the monthly maintenance fees are and what they include; whether there are restrictions on pets, the age of residents, or renting out a unit; and whether there have been recent sales in the building. In addition, tell all potential buyers what is included in the price. For example, let them know if there is a storage locker included, one or two parking spaces, recreational facilities, and so on.

Don't get caught not knowing about your own home. Buyers are hungry for information and they want it fast! They expect that you know about your property unless you are an absentee owner or an investor. If you don't know the answer to their question, the next best thing is to be honest about it and tell buyers that you will find out and let them know as soon as possible. Never give buyers inaccurate information. In real estate, honesty is the only policy!

If you are selling a condo in a new development, you are also selling the builder's and developer's reputation and goodwill. Be sure to mention other projects they are currently building, site builder/developer warrantees, the name of the warrantee holder, after-sales service the builder/developer offers, and reports of customer satisfaction. Potential buyers may be new to the area, province, or country, and they may not know of the builder's or developer's credentials. Include this information as part of your sales and marketing effort.

Equally important for potential buyers are the amenities provided in your condo development. For example, many strata corporations offer recreational facilities — a fitness gym, sauna, hot tub, swimming pool, tennis court, or outdoor areas such as a pond or a lake, or indoor rooms such as a library, sitting room, party room, billiards room, or movie-screening room. In addition, there may be other services that your condominium provides, such as a 24-hour, seven-day-a-week concierge, caretaker, or property manager, or parking facilities for guests and visitors.

Some newly built condominiums offer state-of-the art security systems, with security cameras, security patrols, access to the elevators and the building only by remote control, and other such features. If this is the case in your condominium, make a point of letting potential buyers know, as these added features greatly enhance the property you are selling.

Selling a Rental Property

A rental property can be an attractive investment. Investors often make their buying decisions based on potential revenue, which means you will need to provide accurate information about rental rates. Rental rates fluctuate the same way property prices do, so providing solid information about rents to investors requires that you keep a close eye on local rates and trends.

If you are not up to date on rental rates, you can suggest that a buyer obtain such information from a property manager or real estate agent with expertise in local rental properties.

Selling an Older Home

An older home is generally less expensive than a new home because the older home's replacement cost — the cost of replacing it with a modern equivalent — is higher. Furthermore, GST does not apply to a resale home unless the house has been renovated substantially. In that case, the tax is applied as if the building were a new house.

An additional advantage of resale homes is that they are usually situated in more established neighbourhoods. This means the landscaping has been done and there may be many trees and foliage. In a settled neighbourhood, you will know who your neighbours are, which can be a selling point for buyers.

The main disadvantage of a resale home is that because it is an older building, maintenance costs will likely be higher than those for a new home. The plumbing and electrical systems may be outdated and may need to be repaired, replaced, or updated. You can engage a professional home inspector to check plumbing and electrical systems and also look for structural problems, such as a leaky basement or roof, and to estimate how much repairs will cost. Older homes that do not need repairs may require some redecoration, renovation, or upgrading

You can either perform repairs, upgrading, and renovation yourself or adjust your price to reflect the condition of the home. If you are using a real estate agent, he or she will be able to determine how to price your home based on the upgrades that need to be done.

Chapter 4
GATHERING DATA AND LEGAL DOCUMENTATION

When you are preparing to sell your home, it is important to gather pertinent information about your home before you put it on the market. You may need to order some of the legal documents ahead of time, but if these documents are valid for a limited time, such as a Form "B" or financial statements, you may want to hold off ordering them until your property has an accepted offer.

Other documents may already be in your possession, and it is simply a matter of searching for them and gathering them together. It's a good idea to stay ahead of the game by making the documents readily available for potential buyers should they ask to review them before or after placing an offer. The following are the main pieces of information and documents you will need:

- Title search
- Mortgage information (the title search will show if there is an outstanding mortgage or clear title to the property)
- Survey certificate (if one is available)
- New home warranty information
- Property condition disclosure statement
- Oil tank removal invoice, certification, documentation, and photos (if applicable)

- Invoices for work done recently (e.g., renovations, repairs, etc.)
- Warranties (for newer appliances and renovations)
- Zoning information
- City assessment
- Recent utility bills

If you are selling a strata title property, you will need the following documents:

- Title search
- Mortgage information (the title search will show if there is an outstanding mortgage or clear title to the property)
- New home warranty (for new condos)
- Property condition disclosure statement
- Warranties for newer appliances
- Form "B" or estoppel certificate
- Minutes from strata meetings and AGM
- Strata plan
- By-laws and house rules
- Amendments to the by-laws
- Co-op shares
- Engineer's report
- Financial statements
- Maintenance fee information
- Zoning information
- City assessment
- Recent utility bills

Checklist 1 at the end of this chapter will help you keep track of the documents you have gathered.

Title Search

A title search will let you and potential buyers know who is registered as the current owner of the property. It will also indicate if any registered mortgages, easements, restrictive covenants, or rights-of-way may affect the use or value of the property in either a positive or negative way.

It is important to do a title search to ensure that you, as a seller, are able to convey title to the buyers on the completion date. If the buyer suffers a loss because you cannot convey title, you (and your agent, if one is involved) can be held liable.

The other reason to do a title search is to ensure "genuine consent" on the part of the buyers. This means that the buyers understand what they are buying and are aware of everything that could affect their title if they buy the property. It is important that the legal interest being sold is either free of any charges or that these charges are disclosed. These might be financial charges, such as mortgages or a builder's lien, certificate of pending litigation, or physical encumbrances, such as easements or rights-of-way, and so on.

There are many items that can be included on a title. If you are using a real estate agent, you can ask him or her how to read the title search. Otherwise, you may want to consult a lawyer. You should know that most title search information is very basic. It will show that there is a charge against the property, for example, but will not show the details of the terms, interest payments, and so on. Sample 1 shows a title search form.

When selling a relatively new home, the warranty may still be in effect.

Survey Certificate

A survey formally establishes the boundaries of the property for a single-family dwelling, ensures that all buildings are within those boundaries, and ensures that your house is situated on your lot and is not encroaching on other properties. A survey certificate is often handed down as a courtesy from one property owner to the next, so you may well have received one when you purchased your home. However, if you have made recent upgrades or additions (such as a deck or garage), you may need to get a new survey certificate. Not all buyers require such a certificate, so don't have a new survey done unless it is requested.

New Home Warranty Information

If you bought your home when it was newly built, the new home warranty may still be in effect. This could be a selling point for buyers. You should have details on the type of warranty, what is covered, what is excluded, and when it expires.

Sample 1
TITLE SEARCH

VANCOUVER   LAND TITLE OFFICE   TITLE NO: __ABC 1234__

FROM TITLE NO: __ABC 1233__

APPLICATION FOR REGISTRATION RECEIVED ON: __15 MAY 20—__

ENTERED ON: __02 JUNE 20—__

REGISTERED OWNER IN FEE SIMPLE:

MR. ABE SMITH, BUSINESSMAN, AND ABELLE SMITH, STUDENT
54321 ANYWHERE STREET, ANYWHERE TOWN

JOINT TENANTS

TAXATION AUTHORITY: __CITY OF VANCOUVER__

DESCRIPTION OF LAND: _____

PARECEL IDENTIFIER: __000-123-333-456__

__LOT 1   BLOCK 2   DISTRICT LOT 4900   PLAN 220__

LEGAL NOTATIONS: __NONE__

CHARGES, LIENS, AND INTERESTS: _____

NATURE OF CHARGE: _____

CHARGE NUMBER: _____ DATE: _____ TIME: _____

MORTGAGE: __DDD00000999   1997-05-01   14:50__

REGISTERED OWNER OF CHARGE: __THE BANK   TF00990__

DUPLICATE INDEFEASIBLE TITLE: __NONE OUTSTANDING__

TRANSFERS: __NONE__

PENDING APPLICATIONS: __NONE__

Property Condition Disclosure Statement (PCDS)

Regulatory bodies and real estate boards throughout North America have introduced property condition disclosure statements (PCDS) to address concerns about health, safety, and environmental protection in relation to homes (see Sample 2). Regulators have set stringent levels for safety, greater disclosure, and broader responsibilities and liabilities in relation to these matters. Buyers, sellers, and current and former owners, as well as the seller's agent, share in that responsibility and potential liability.

Possible health risks related to your property should be disclosed on PCDS forms.

The intent of a PCDS is to properly document the history of the property and its current condition, in writing. It is signed by the seller and dated. The PCDS deals with environmental, structural, and mechanical issues, as well as water, sewage, plumbing, and renovations information. It provides the seller with written proof that the deficiencies or defects were disclosed to the buyer and that the buyer knew of these deficiencies. It is usually part of the contract of purchase and sale if both the seller and the buyer agree to this in writing.

A PCDS should be current and accurate. Unfortunately, disclosure statements that are filled in and signed by property investors are not as accurate as those provided by owners who have occupied the property. Because the owners of the investment properties have not lived in the properties, they may not be aware of the problems in the unit or building.

In past decades, asbestos insulation and urea formaldehyde foam insulation (UFFI) have attracted interest as possible health risks. Recently, the presence of radon gas, lead pipes, and even lead-based paint, found in older properties, has been a concern to buyers. These issues are covered on the PCDS forms.

Another area of concern, which is rarely disclosed, is information on crime statistics or the location of an ex-convict. In Alberta, the RCMP has developed a public website that discloses the location of some sex offenders. Where such data banks exist, home sellers (and real estate professionals on behalf of their clients) have a duty to check them. The guiding principle is that you must disclose anything that could, in the mind of a reasonable buyer, affect the use, enjoyment, and/or perceived value of the property.

If you know about a problem and do not reveal it to a buyer, or if you misrepresent a property by falsifying documents, the

PROPERTY CONDITION DISCLOSURE STATEMENT

PROPERTY CONDITION DISCLOSURE STATEMENT

The Seller is responsible for disclosing to the buyer any and all material facts about the property. This form is intended to aid the Seller in this duty and to aid the Buyer in his or her evaluation of the property. The Seller is responsible for the accuracy of the information provided herein, and verifies that it is true to the best of his or her knowledge and complies with local regulations.

Date: _____

Address of property: _____

Seller must initial appropriate column

		Yes	No	Don't know	N/A
1.	Is the property connected to a public sewer system?	[ ]	[ ]	[ ]	[ ]
2.	Is the property connected to a public water system?	[ ]	[ ]	[ ]	[ ]
3.	Does the water system have any known defects?	[ ]	[ ]	[ ]	[ ]
4.	Does the septic system have any known defects?	[ ]	[ ]	[ ]	[ ]
5.	Is the property connected to a private water system or serviced by a private well?	[ ]	[ ]	[ ]	[ ]
6.	Does the property now have or has it ever had an underground oil storage tank?	[ ]	[ ]	[ ]	[ ]
7.	Are there currently or have there ever been toxic substances stored on the property?	[ ]	[ ]	[ ]	[ ]
8.	Has the property ever contained asbestos insulation?	[ ]	[ ]	[ ]	[ ]
9.	Has the property ever contained formaldehyde insulation?	[ ]	[ ]	[ ]	[ ]
10.	Is the ceiling insulated?	[ ]	[ ]	[ ]	[ ]
11.	Are the exterior walls insulated?	[ ]	[ ]	[ ]	[ ]
12.	Are you aware of any structural defects of the premises?	[ ]	[ ]	[ ]	[ ]
13.	Are there problems with any of the following:				
	* heating and/or air conditioning systems	[ ]	[ ]	[ ]	[ ]
	* fireplace(s)	[ ]	[ ]	[ ]	[ ]
	* electrical system	[ ]	[ ]	[ ]	[ ]
	* plumbing system	[ ]	[ ]	[ ]	[ ]
	* hot tub and/or swimming pool	[ ]	[ ]	[ ]	[ ]
	* rodents and/or insects	[ ]	[ ]	[ ]	[ ]
	* mould	[ ]	[ ]	[ ]	[ ]
	* leakage or moisture	[ ]	[ ]	[ ]	[ ]
14.	Are you aware of any damage due to fire, water, or wind?	[ ]	[ ]	[ ]	[ ]
15.	Has this house ever been used as a marijuana grow operation or a crystal meth laboratory?	[ ]	[ ]	[ ]	[ ]
16.	Does the roof leak or has it ever been damaged?	[ ]	[ ]	[ ]	[ ]
17.	How old is the roof? _____ years	[ ]	[ ]	[ ]	[ ]
18.	Has the property ever been flooded?	[ ]	[ ]	[ ]	[ ]
19.	Is the property subject to any easements, rights of way, or shared-use agreements?	[ ]	[ ]	[ ]	[ ]
20.	Have you received notice of any claim against the property?	[ ]	[ ]	[ ]	[ ]
21.	Are there any legal actions pending that may affect the property?	[ ]	[ ]	[ ]	[ ]
22.	Are you aware of any additions, alterations, or renovations made to the property?	[ ]	[ ]	[ ]	[ ]
23.	Has a final building inspection been approved or a final occupancy permit been obtained?	[ ]	[ ]	[ ]	[ ]
24.	Are there any disclosures not covered above?	[ ]	[ ]	[ ]	[ ]

Comments (attach additional pages if necessary):

_____

_____

_____

Additional clauses specific to strata/condo units	Yes	No	Don't know	N/A
25. Are there any special assessments proposed or voted on? (If yes, provide information below.)	[ ]	[ ]	[ ]	[ ]
26. Are there any restrictions regarding the following:				
* pets	[ ]	[ ]	[ ]	[ ]
* rentals	[ ]	[ ]	[ ]	[ ]
* age	[ ]	[ ]	[ ]	[ ]
* TV antennas/satellite dishes	[ ]	[ ]	[ ]	[ ]
* parking for guests	[ ]	[ ]	[ ]	[ ]
27. Are the following documents available:				
* by-laws	[ ]	[ ]	[ ]	[ ]
* current year operating budget	[ ]	[ ]	[ ]	[ ]
* current year financial statements	[ ]	[ ]	[ ]	[ ]
* strata council meeting minutes for last 12 months, including extraordinary meetings and AGM	[ ]	[ ]	[ ]	[ ]
28. What is the monthly maintenance fee? $_____	[ ]	[ ]	[ ]	[ ]
29. Does unit come with parking stall?	[ ]	[ ]	[ ]	[ ]
30. Does unit come with storage locker?	[ ]	[ ]	[ ]	[ ]

Comments (attach additional pages if necessary):

_____

_____

_____

The seller(s) acknowledges that the information provided on this form is true and complete to the best of his or her knowledge as of the date on page 1. Any additional information or amendments to the above information that may arise will be disclosed to the buyer prior to closing. The seller acknowledges receipt of a copy of this form and agrees that a copy may be provided to the buyer.

_____   _____
Seller's signature   *Seller's signature*

_____   _____
Print name   *Print name*

The buyer(s) acknowledges receipt of a copy of this form. The buyer also acknowledges his or her own obligation to examine the property to verify all material facts, and that he or she should also have a property inspection done by a professional, independent third party.

_____   _____
Buyer's signature   *Buyer's signature*

_____   _____
Print name   *Print name*

This form is not intended as a warranty or guarantee of any kind.

Buyers must assess whether the property they are purchasing is a high risk or not.

buyer can sue you under the common laws of agency, contract, and negligence. If you are not aware of a problem — if, for example, you are selling a rental property and are not a hands-on owner or live in another city (i.e., you use a property management company to handle the rentals), then you may not be entirely liable. If you are in doubt, seek the advice of legal counsel immediately.

Many provinces and municipalities have their own disclosure statement forms, as areas of concern may vary from one area to another. You can obtain a PCDS form that addresses issues pertinent to your area from your local real estate board. (See Appendix 1 for a list of real estate associations and boards by province.)

Buyers are expected to do their own due diligence to find out whether the property they are purchasing is a high risk or not. The purchase of any home has some risk, and it is up to buyers to look at these risks and figure out whether they are comfortable with them. They should confirm the statements in a PCDS by, for example, inquiring about renovations or improvements to ascertain when they were done. If you state that the roof shingles were replaced two years ago, buyers may check the date by asking to look at the invoice or by contacting the roofer. Some building inspectors read PCDSs and take the time to verify or deny what has been written.

If you are unwilling to fill out a property condition disclosure statement, many buyers will simply walk away from your property. They may assume you are hiding something. Others will hire a qualified inspector to perform a full inspection of the property. If you are using a real estate agent, he or she may not be able to post the listing on the local real estate board's multiple listing service. Some boards and associations have made completion of a PCDS mandatory for every real estate listing.

Oil Tank Removal

Many underground heating-oil tanks have reached the end of their useful lives and are beginning to corrode, rust, and leak. If you have had your oil tank removed, this should be mentioned in your disclosure statement. This is a positive feature, as most buyers would want this problem dealt with, either by having the price reduced or by having the oil tank removed before they purchase the property.

If you have had the tank removed, potential buyers need to know when this work was done and the name of the oil tank removal company. They will likely want to see the following documents:

- A copy of the oil tank removal certification.
- Photographs documenting the removal.
- A report from the oil tank company stating that there were no signs of oil contamination.
- A certificate from the fire department stating that the soil in the surrounding area was not contaminated.

You should check with your city or municipality about local codes and regulations regarding oil tanks. A real estate agent can also help you with this and can provide a list of contact names and numbers for companies in your area that remove oil tanks. There is also a resource list in Appendix 2.

Revealing the amount of property taxes you pay will let buyers know whether they can afford to purchase your home.

Zoning Information

Local governments designate zones for certain areas to specify the types of buildings that may be built on particular properties and how those buildings may be used. For example, there could be single-family or multi-family residential, duplex, commercial, or industrial structures. Look for zoning information on your title and include this in the information that you provide potential buyers.

City Assessment

Revealing the amount of property taxes you pay will let buyers know whether they can afford to purchase your home. If you do not have the current year's tax bill available, see the city assessment to calculate the annual property taxes.

Restrictions

If you are selling a strata title property or a home in a new development, you must inform potential buyers of any restrictions on the property. Go through the strata corporation by-laws, rules, regulations, and amendments to the by-laws to find restrictions or prohibitions imposed on an owner's ability to rent or use the property.

Strata corporations may place restrictions on some or all of the following aspects:

- **Age of residents:** A development may specify that it is for adults only.

- **Rental:** There may be only a limited number of units that can be rented, or an owner may need the strata council's permission to rent.

- **Pets:** There may be rules specifying the size, weight, number, and type of pets you can have in a unit, or pets may be prohibited.

- **Use:** Regulations may specify what activities cannot take place on the property (such as running a business or an illegal activity).

- **Window coverings:** The building may have set a uniform colour for window coverings.

- **Waterbeds:** Waterbeds may be prohibited in the building, they may be restricted to a certain location within a unit, or owners may need to have proof of damage insurance if they want to install a waterbed.

- **Hot tubs:** Hot tubs may be prohibited on roof decks because of potential damage from leaks or weight problems.

- **Hardwood floors:** Especially in frame buildings, hardwood floors may be prohibited because of noise.

- **Christmas trees:** Live trees may not be acceptable as they may cause fire in the building.

Restrictions are not necessarily a negative issue for home-buyers. For example, restrictions that limit or prohibit rentals may be a positive factor for buyers. The fact that the people living in a building own their units generally has a positive impact.

Other Information for Strata Property

The Form "B" or estoppel certificate, issued by the property management company, indicates how much money is in the contingency or reserve fund.

Minutes from strata council meetings document issues and business dealings that have come up in relation to the property. For example, they may cover discussions about maintenance and repair programs for the upkeep of a building.

By-laws specify how a condominium establishes its house rules and restrictions. By-laws are made, amended, or repealed by the board of directors. They are not effective unless the owners of the majority of units vote in favour.

If the home you are selling is part of a co-operative, you will be transferring co-op shares rather than land. You should have a copy of your share certificate, which indicates how many shares you hold, as well as any particulars concerning the rights that are for sale, such as the suite location and other exclusive areas.

An engineer's report, prepared by a professional engineering company, will give details of the structure of the building, the building envelope, and the foundation of the building. Some reports will include recommendations on work that should be done and price estimates.

Financial statements indicate revenue (funds generated from monthly maintenance fees) and expenses (such as maintenance costs and management costs). They are prepared by the condominium corporation for each fiscal period.

Maintenance fees paid by owners of condos, townhouses, and detached houses in developments cover the costs of insurance, management, and upkeep of common property. In some instances they may also include the cost of gas and hot water and/or yearly taxes. It is important that you list details of these maintenance fees in any information you hand out to potential buyers. If you are not sure what is included in maintenance fees for your strata property, call your property management company for details.

Other Documentation

If recent renovations or new appliances are selling points for your property, you should have invoices available so buyers can see exactly when work was done or when appliances were purchased. You should also have copies of any warranties still in force for renovations or appliances. Recent utility bills will indicate how much a buyer should expect to pay for electricity, heating, etc. If you have copies of maintenance records for equipment included in the purchase, such as a gas fireplace, furnace, sprinkler system, hot water tank, air conditioner, or applicances, you may want to make these available to the buyer as well.

Measuring Your Property

It is important that you know your home and property's measurements, as many buyers will ask for the dimensions of your home

and of each room in your home so that they can determine whether it will satisfy their needs. You can do the measuring yourself, but it may be a good idea to hire a professional measurement company to assist you. Include the warning "Buyers to verify their own measurements" in all literature you hand out so that buyers will perform their own due diligence by measuring room sizes themselves, if it is important to them.

If you are doing the measuring yourself, be aware that you measure only the total finished area of the building. In residential buildings, do not include porches, decks, and patios (whether they are closed in, screened in, or open); garages or carports; crawl spaces and areas underneath dormers; or other unfinished areas situated below grade (underground). These areas should be listed separately on your information sheet under a description of the property.

According to the Standard Measurement Committee of the Canadian Real Estate Association, you should take measurements from the outside surface of the exterior walls for detached houses; from the centre line of the party walls for row houses; and from the outside surface of exterior walls and the centre line of party walls for semi-detached houses and end units of row housing.

If you are selling a condo, you should *not* include balconies, large patios, or parking stalls in the condominium measurements. Instead, look at your strata plan for information. It is best to define the condominium by reference to the walls of the buildings. Developers, in an attempt to increase the apparent size of a condominium unit, have often included outside areas, such as balconies and large patios, in their measurements, but these are in fact part of the common property, with each unit owner having exclusive use of these areas.

When you advertise your condo, you should indicate the square area of the condominium, together with any exclusive-use areas, as in the following example: "This condominium is 112.59 m^2, together with exclusive use of patio, large balcony, and one parking space." This defines what is being offered and eliminates confusion about the measurement of condominiums.

If you are ever in doubt about how or what to measure, you can opt to hire a professional management company to measure your home. This ensures that the information you are providing potential buyers is accurate.

Pre-Sale Building Inspection

Until recently, when properties went on the market, the common practice was that a buyer made an offer "subject to approving and being satisfied with a building inspection." After the building inspection, the seller suddenly learned about various problems. He or she may not have known about them or may have been somewhat aware of them but was not being completely upfront about these problems.

To avoid such surprises, more and more sellers are opting to have a pre-sale home inspection done before they list their home. This is an out-of-pocket expense for the seller, but it is worth the cost for the peace of mind it gives you. Such an inspection will identify problems you may not know about, but which would show up in a buyer's inspection. If you know of these problems ahead of time, you can either adjust the price accordingly or fix the problems before the house goes on the market. Sample 3 shows an inspection summary report, which will give you a general idea of the types of things a building inspector looks at.

Arranging for a pre-sale inspection not only helps you determine a fair market price for your home, but also shows buyers that you are being upfront, fair, and honest in representing your property.

The Canadian Association of Home and Property Inspectors <www.cahi.ca> represents the existing provincial inspection association and oversees a national standard of competency for the industry. Provincial associations are listed in Table 2.

INSPECTION SUMMARY

Inspection Summary

Inspection address:_____ Date:_____

Note: This summary is intended to provide an overview of the condition of the major systems inspected. Where possible the inspector has included some maintenance tips and improvement ideas in the body of the report. The client is encouraged to keep and review the complete report. All homes require regular maintenance.

The results of this report are from a visual survey performed for the sole, confidential & exclusive use of the client noted on page 1. No inspection of hidden or concealed items has been made, therefore no opinion can be expressed on these items. The results of this inspection are opinion and there is NO ATTACHED OR IMPLIED GUARANTEE OR WARRANTY. This report is NOT to be relied on by any third party.

❏   Specialists' reports are recommended for:

❏ Fire sprinkler system	❏ Pool/spa system	❏ Septic system	❏ Foundation
❏ Security alarm system	❏ Underground oil tank	❏ Well + water	❏

Major Systems Condition Overview

	Functional	Suggest maintenance	Repair or replace	Other comments	
Site Conditions	❏	❏	❏	❏	_____
Garage/Carport	❏	❏	❏	❏	_____
Interior Walls	❏	❏	❏	❏	_____
Exterior Doors & Windows	❏	❏	❏	❏	_____
Porches, Decks & Balconies	❏	❏	❏	❏	_____
Roofing	❏	❏	❏	❏	_____
Attic & Insulation	❏	❏	❏	❏	_____
Interior Walls, Ceilings & Floors	❏	❏	❏	❏	_____
Kitchen	❏	❏	❏	❏	_____
Bathrooms	❏	❏	❏	❏	_____
Laundry Facilities	❏	❏	❏	❏	_____
Fireplace	❏	❏	❏	❏	_____
Foundation	❏	❏	❏	❏	_____
Basement/Crawlspace	❏	❏	❏	❏	_____
Structure	❏	❏	❏	❏	_____
Plumbing	❏	❏	❏	❏	_____
Heating	❏	❏	❏	❏	_____
Ventilation	❏	❏	❏	❏	_____
Electrical	❏	❏	❏	❏	_____

Comments:

_____
_____
_____
_____
_____
_____

Table 2
PROVINCIAL ASSOCIATIONS OF HOME AND PROPERTY INSPECTORS

Province	Acronym	Website
British Columbia	CAHPI-BC	www.cahpi.bc.ca
Alberta	CAHPT-AB	www.cahpi-alberta.com
Saskatchewan	CAHPI-SASK	www.cahpi-sk.com
Manitoba	CAHPI-MB	www.cahi.mb.ca
Ontario	OAHI	www.oahi.com
Quebec	AIBC	www.aibq.qc.ca
Atlantic Provinces	CAHPI-ATL	www.cahpiatl.com

Checklist 1
DOCUMENTS AND INFORMATION

The following are the main pieces of information and documents you will need:

- ❑ Title search
- ❑ Mortgage information (the title search will show if there is an outstanding mortgage or clear title to property)
- ❑ Survey certificate (if one is available)
- ❑ New home warranty information
- ❑ Property condition disclosure statement
- ❑ Oil tank (if applicable):
    - ❑ removal invoice
    - ❑ certification
    - ❑ documentation
    - ❑ photos
- ❑ Invoices for work done recently:
    - ❑ renovations _____
    - ❑ repairs _____
    - ❑ maintenance report _____
- ❑ Warranties:
    - ❑ appliances _____
    - ❑ renovations _____
    - ❑ other_____
- ❑ Zoning information
- ❑ City assessment
- ❑ Recent utility bills:
    - ❑ hydro
    - ❑ electric
    - ❑ cable
    - ❑ telephone
    - ❑ other_____
    - ❑ other_____

Checklist 1 — Continued

You will need the following documents if you are selling a strata title property:

❏ Title search

❏ Mortgage information (the title search will show if there is an outstanding mortgage or clear title to property)

❏ New home warranty (for new condos)

❏ Property condition disclosure statement

❏ Warranties:

    ❏ appliances _____

    ❏ renovations _____

    ❏ other _____

❏ Form "B" or estoppel certificate

❏ Minutes from strata meetings and AGM

❏ Strata plan

❏ By-laws and house rules

❏ Amendments to house rules and by-laws

❏ Co-op shares

❏ Engineer's report

❏ Financial statements

❏ Maintenance fee information

❏ Zoning information

❏ City assessment

❏ Recent utility bills:

    ❏ hydro

    ❏ electric

    ❏ cable

    ❏ telephone

    ❏ other _____

    ❏ other _____

Chapter 5
SELLING YOUR HOME: WHAT IS IT WORTH?

Why Are You Selling?

One of the key questions that buyers will ask is your reason for selling, your motivation. Perhaps you have or your spouse has been transferred to a job in a new city or province. Maybe you have gone through a divorce and want to make a new start somewhere else, or you have to sell the house as part of a divorce settlement. Or you might just want to move to a bigger or smaller house, depending on the stage of life you are at. If you are moving for personal reasons that you do not want to disclose, talk to your agent about the best way to withhold personal information.

However, if your motivation has to do with the property itself — for example, if the condominium you purchased has a special assessment forthcoming, or your house needs major renovations that you don't want to do yourself — the guiding principle to remember is: Any information that may negatively affect a buyer's decision to purchase must be made known to him or her.

What Is Your Home Worth?

There are two basic ways to find out how much your home is worth in today's market — in other words, its market value. You can

engage a real estate agent to provide you with a Comparative Market Analysis (CMA), or you can hire an appraiser to help you determine the value of your home. Many agents will provide this service for free in the hope that they will establish a rapport with you and you will list with them or will refer them to friends or family. An appraiser will charge you for the service.

Agents determine what the home is worth by looking at active, sold, and expired listings in the area and base their price on what the market is doing over a short period of time, say three months in an active market. Appraisers work for the banks and make their evaluation of what a home is worth based on land values, the home's condition, etc. In general, appraisers tend to be on the conservative side when providing a value to a home, and it may differ from the purchase price that buyers are willing to pay at a given point in time. In short, the difference between an appraiser and an agent is that appraisers provide sellers with an estimate of what their home is worth, while agents indicate what the market is willing to pay. Sample 4 shows a summary appraisal report form.

It is not a good idea to price your property yourself without an appraiser or an agent to provide you with crucial data and information about market statistics. Many sellers, when they see that their neighbour's home sold for a specific price, want that exact same price (or better) for their home. However, each property is unique, and each property's value will depend on many factors such as age of the home, square footage, upgrades to kitchen, bathroom, electrical, or plumbing, and so on.

Though you can use the Internet to get an idea of how much homes in your area are selling for, it is always a good idea to ask for professional help to get the best price for your home.

What is a comparative market analysis (CMA)?

A comparative market analysis (CMA) is a comparison of similar properties that have recently been sold. It operates on the principle of substitution, assuming that the market value of the subject property is equivalent to prices recently paid for similar properties. The CMA method is most useful for properties that are similar within their property class, such as single-family dwellings or condominium units. It may not be useful for properties such as industrial or commercial buildings.

When the CMA is used for single-family dwellings, it compares your property with others of the same age, square footage, lot size,

Sample 4
SUMMARY APPRAISAL REPORT

SUMMARY APPRAISAL REPORT
HOME OWNERSHIP UNITS

CLIENT: _____

_____ Complete _____ Limited
ADDRESS OF PROPERTY

APPRAISER _____

ADDRESS: _____

ADDRESS: _____

TEL: (____) _____

CITY _____

PROVINCE _____ POSTAL CODE _____

TEL: (____) _____

APPLICANT NAME
LEGAL DESCRIPTION _____

MUNICIPALITY or DISTRICT _____
ASSESSMENT: LAND _____ IMP _____ TOTAL _____ TAXES $ _____ YEAR _____
PURPOSE OF APPRAISAL: To estimate the market value _____ or _____
INTENDED USE OF APPRAISAL: Financing _____ or _____
PROPERTY RIGHTS APPRAISED: Fee simple _____ Leasehold _____ Condominium _____ Co-operative _____ Other (Specify) _____
OCCUPIED BY: Owner _____ Tenant _____ Vacant _____
HIGHEST & BEST USE: As Improved _____ NOTE: IF HIGHEST & BEST USE IS NOT THE CURRENT USE - SEE COMMENTS

NEIGHBOURHOOD DESCRIPTION

NATURE OF DISTRICT	TREND OF DISTRICT	CONFORMITY OF SUBJ.	AVG. AGE OF PROPERTIES IN NEIGHBOURHOOD:	SUPPLY	DEMAND
RESIDENTIAL	IMPROVING	INFERIOR		GOOD	GOOD
RURAL	STABLE	SIMILAR	_____ YEARS	FAIR	FAIR
MIXED	DETERIORATING	SUPERIOR	AREA BUILT UP _____ %	POOR	POOR
	TRANSITION				

DISTANCE TO ELEMENTARY SCHOOL _____ PUBLIC TRANSPORTATION _____ PRICE RANGE IN NEIGHBOURHOOD
SECONDARY SCHOOL _____ SHOPPING FACILITIES _____ $ _____
DOWNTOWN _____

SUMMARY: including VALUE TRENDS AND ADVERSE INFLUENCES IN AREA, if any (e.g., railroad tracks, commercial/industrial properties, unkempt properties, major traffic arteries, etc.)

SITE DESCRIPTION

SITE DIMENSIONS: _____
SITE AREA: _____ SOURCE: _____
TOPOGRAPHY: _____
CONFIGURATION: _____
ZONING: _____

_____ PAVED ROAD
_____ GRAVEL ROAD
_____ SIDEWALK
_____ CURBS
_____ STREET LIGHTS
_____ CABLEVISION

_____ TELEPHONE
_____ GAS
_____ MUNICIPAL WATER
_____ WELL—PRIVATE
_____ WELL—COMMUNAL

_____ SANITARY SEWER
_____ SEPTIC
_____ STORM SEWER
_____ OPEN DITCH

DOES PRESENT USE CONFORM: _____ YES _____ NO IF NO, SEE COMMENTS.

LANDSCAPING		EASEMENTS	DRIVEWAY				ELECTRICAL
EXCELLENT	FAIR	UTILITY	PRIVATE	SINGLE	CONCRETE		UNDERGROUND
GOOD	POOR	ACCESS	MUTUAL	DOUBLE	ASPHALT		OVERHEAD
AVERAGE	NONE		NONE				

COMMENT ON ANY POSITIVE/NEGATIVE FEATURES: (e.g., regarding conforming of zoning, effects of easements, etc.)

DESCRIPTION OF IMPROVEMENTS — EXTERIOR

ESTIMATED YEAR BUILT: _____
CONSTRUCTION COMPLETE: _____
EFFECTIVE AGE: _____
PERCENTAGE COMPLETE: _____
ESTIMATED REMAINING LIFE (Yrs.) _____
HOLDBACK RECOMMENDED: _____

FLOOR AREA	BASEMENT	TYPE OF BUILDING	DESIGN	CONSTRUCTION
SOURCE _____	_____ FULL	_____ DETACHED	_____ ONE-STOREY	_____ WOOD FRAME
MAIN _____	_____ PARTIAL	_____ SEMI-DETACHED	_____ SPLIT-LEVEL	_____ BRICK
2nd _____	_____ CRAWL SPACE	_____ ROW/TOWNHOUSE	_____ 1 1/2 STOREY	_____ STONE
3rd _____	TOTAL AREA _____	APARTMENT _____	_____ 2-STOREY	_____ CONCRETE
TOTAL _____	_____ SQ.FT. _____ SQ.M.			
SQ.FT. _____ SQ.M.	EXTERIOR FINISH		ROOFING MATERIAL	OVERALL EXT. CONDITION
WINDOW SASH/GLAZING	_____ BRICK VENEER	_____ WOOD SIDING	_____ ASPHALT SHINGLE	_____ GOOD
	_____ SOLID BRICK	_____ ALUMINUM	_____ WOOD SHINGLE	_____ AVERAGE
	_____ STONE VENEER	_____ VINYL	_____ TAR & GRAVEL	_____ FAIR
U.F.F.I. APPARENT _____ YES	_____ SOLID STONE	_____ INSULBRICK		_____ POOR
_____ NO	_____ STUCCO		APPROX. AGE _____	

DESCRIPTION OF IMPROVEMENTS — INTERIOR

INSULATION	FLOORING		WALLS	CEILINGS	FINISH
_____ CEILING	_____ W-W CARPET	_____ SHEET VINYL			_____ PLYWOOD
_____ WALLS	_____ SOFTWOOD	_____ VINYL TILE			_____ PLASTER
_____ BASEMENT	_____ HARDWOOD	_____ CERAMIC			_____ GYPSUM BOARD
_____ CRAWL	_____ LINOLEUM				

FLOOR PLAN	CLOSETS	BEDROOMS (#)	BATHROOMS (#)		OVERALL INT. CONDITION
_____ GOOD	_____ GOOD	_____ LARGE	_____ 2-Pc.	_____ GOOD	_____ GOOD
_____ AVERAGE	_____ AVERAGE	_____ AVERAGE	_____ 3-Pc.	_____ AVERAGE	_____ AVERAGE
_____ FAIR	_____ FAIR	_____ SMALL	_____ 4-Pc.	_____ POOR	_____ FAIR
_____ POOR	_____ POOR		_____ 5-Pc.	_____ CUSTOM	_____ POOR

Form#: CSA-USPAP 08/97 Page 1

This form was produced using CRAL™ for Windows 1-800-CSA-5550

Client Reference No:

FOUNDATION WALLS	PLUMBING LINES	ELECTRICAL	WATER HEATER	File No: HEATING SYSTEM
POURED CONCRETE	COPPER	FUSES	GAS	FORCED AIR
CONCRETE BLOCK	PVC OR PLASTIC	BREAKERS	ELECTRIC	BASEBOARD
CONCRETE SLAB	GALVANIZED			HOT WATER
BRICK OR STONE		RATED CAPACITY OF MAIN	CAPACITY	
		BREAKERS _____ AMPS		FUEL TYPE

BUILT-IN APPLIANCES/EXTRA FEATURES:

STOVE	VACUUM	CENTRAL AIR	SAUNA	SOLARIUM
OVEN	GARBAGE DISPOSAL	AIR CLEANER	WHIRLPOOL	SKYLIGHTS
DISHWASHER	FIREPLACE(S)	SECURITY SYSTEM	SWIMMING POOL	GARAGE OPENER

BASEMENT FINISHES, UTILITY:

GARAGES/CARPORTS:

DECKS, PATIOS, OTHER IMPROVEMENTS:

COMMENTS: Building appearance, quality, condition, services, including extras:

ROOM ALLOCATION / COST APPROACH

LEVEL:	MAIN	SECOND	THIRD		BSMT.
ROOMS:					
ENTRANCE					
LIVING					
DINING					
KITCHEN					
FULL BATH					
PART BATH					
BEDROOM					
FAMILY					
LAUNDRY					
OTHER(S)					

COST APPROACH

SOURCE OF COST DATA: _____ MANUAL _____ LOCAL CONTRACTOR _____ OTHER

LAND VALUE: .... $

BUILDING   COST NEW   DEPRECIATED COST

COST ....@ $ _____ $ _____ $ _____

GARAGE: $ _____ $ _____

BASEMENT FINISH:..................

OTHER EXTRAS $ _____ $ _____

  $ _____ $ _____

  $ _____ $ _____

  $ _____ $ _____

TOTAL REPLACEMENT COST: $ _____

LESS: ACCRUED DEPRECIATION _____ % $ _____ $ _____

INDICATED VALUE: ....

VALUE BY THE COST APPROACH (rounded) .... $

DIRECT COMPARISON APPROACH

ITEM	SUBJECT PROPERTY	COMPARABLE NO. 1 DESCRIPTION	$ ADJUST.	COMPARABLE NO. 2 DESCRIPTION	$ ADJUST.	COMPARABLE NO. 3 DESCRIPTION	$ ADJUST.
ADDRESS							
DATE OF SALE							
SALE PRICE							
SITE SIZE							
SIZE L.F.A.							
AGE/CONDITION	/	/		/		/	
STYLE							
RMS/BEDS/BATHS	/ /	/ /	/ /	/ /	/ /		
BASEMENT	Sq.Ft.						
GARAGE/PARKING							
ADJUSTED VALUES/NET ADJUSTED TOTALS							

CONCLUSIONS:

VALUE BY THE DIRECT COMPARISON APPROACH (ROUNDED) $

FINAL ESTIMATE OF VALUE/COMMENT ON REASONABLE EXPOSURE TIME:

COMMENT ON AND ANALYZE ANY KNOWN SALES, LISTING, OR OFFER TO PURCHASE ON THE SUBJECT PROPERTY OVER THE PAST YEAR:
(Include source of information.)

AS A RESULT OF MY APPRAISAL AND ANALYSIS IT IS MY OPINION THAT THE MARKET VALUE OF THE SUBJECT PROPERTY AS AT _____ IS $ _____ THIS REPORT WAS COMPLETED ON _____

[X] TITLE PAGE	[ ] AREA CALCULATIONS	[X] MAP ADDENDUM	[ ] ENVIRONMENTAL ADDENDUM	[X] CERTIFICATION	[ ]
[ ] REPORT PROFILE	[ ] SKETCH ADDENDUM	[X] PHOTO ADDENDA	[X] SCOPE OF APPRAISAL	[ ] SCHEDULE A/NARRATIVE	[ ]
[ ] TRANSMITTAL LETTER	[ ] COMPS 4-5-6	[ ] NARRATIVE ADDENDUM	[ ] USPAP DEPARTURE DISCLOSURE	[X] INVOICE FOR SERVICES	[ ]

APPRAISER
SIGNATURE _____ DESIGNATION _____
NAME _____ INSPECTED PROP. (DATE) _____

SUPERVISOR
SIGNATURE _____ DESIGNATION _____
NAME _____ INSPECTED PROP. (DATE) _____

Form#: CSA-USPAP 08/97 Page 2   This form was produced using CRAL™ for Windows 1-800-CSA-5550

and so on, in the same neighbourhood. For condominiums, a comparison is made with active, sold, and expired listings in the same building, with the same characteristics as the property being compared. That is, one-bedroom units are compared with other one-bedroom properties with similar areas in the same building. (If there are no similar listings in your building with recent sales, the agent will make a comparison with similar buildings in the area.) A single detached home will not be compared with an apartment or townhouse as they are not in the same class. In other words, apples are compared with other apples and not oranges.

A CMA allows agents to get the most accurate comparisons for similar properties with the same basic parameters, such as the same square footage, the same number of bedrooms and bathrooms, the same general age, amenities, frontage and depth (for single detached homes), and so on.

An agent prepares a CMA report by collecting and analyzing market sales data for all of the similar properties sold in the previous six months to a year. He or she will also look at the market conditions and at active and expired listings within the same time frame to determine the best value for your home. Sample 5 at the end of this chapter is an example of a CMA.

In addition to the CMA, agents will look for items that bring added value to your home. In a condominium, the following things can fetch a premium price:

- Location on a higher or top floor
- Water or city view
- Balcony
- Gas fireplace
- In-suite laundry
- Double or triple glazed windows
- Bay windows
- In-suite storage
- Soaker tub
- Stainless steel appliances
- Skylights
- Fitness centre in building
- Wheelchair access
- Security cameras

Agents collect and analyze sales data to determine the best price for your property.

For a detached home, features that have a positive impact on value include:

- Front yard
- Backyard
- Fenced property
- Hardwood floors
- Landscaping
- Multi-vehicle garage
- Location on a quiet street

Agents will also look for items that decrease your home's value. The following features have a negative impact on the value of a home:

- Lack of access to public transportation
- Distance from public transportation
- Location near an industrial building
- Location behind a commercial property
- Location behind or beside a condominium
- An oil tank on the property
- The home once housed a marijuana grow operation or produced other drugs
- Location on a "T" street
- No back lane
- Near or under electrical lines
- Irregular-shaped lot

An agent will establish a price range for fair market value. However, this is not an exact science, because each property is unique. If you are selling a condominium, for example, another property in the same building, even on the same floor, may be valued higher or lower. An agent will be able to tell you exactly why a certain unit in a condominium or a certain home in a particular neighbourhood sold for $10,000 more than another property in the same building or neighbourhood. Perhaps one property was on a lower floor, or it did not have a view or updated appliances.

Another factor affecting the accuracy of a CMA is that agents are not aware of all properties sold, such as houses for sale by owner (FSBO).

There is a time limit for a CMA. If you have one done but don't list your house for sale right away, chances are the market will have changed. Even a month or two later, your original CMA may not reflect the current market and you will need to have a new one done.

Obtaining a CMA is important from the buyer's point of view, as most lending institutions will require an appraisal of your property. The appraised value may affect the amount of the loan the buyer can get.

Increasing or decreasing your price

If your home has been on the market for a while and has not sold, or if you have not had any offers, you should consider changing the price you are asking. It may be that the market has changed and prices have dropped, or there may be more or better inventory (i.e., houses or condos) for sale. You can obtain a more recent CMA and adjust the price to reflect the market. Most agents update their clients' CMAs on a regular basis to make sure they are in touch with the market and have priced their homes accordingly.

It is not uncommon for sellers to increase or decrease their price. They could make a change for a number of reasons:

- If the price was more than or less than fair market value to begin with.

- If the market has changed from a buyer's to a seller's market or vice versa. For example, if it has become a buyer's market and there are a lot of properties on the market, you might want to decrease your price so your property is more attractive to buyers. If it is a seller's market, with few properties competing with yours, you may want to increase your price.

- If you have already been relocated or have already placed an offer on another property, you may want to sell faster to avoid having to apply for bridge financing.

- If it is a "soft" market, without too much activity, as often happens during the fall and winter, you may want to lower the price.

If you list your property on the MLS system, buyers are aware of the listing date, so they know if a property has been on the market for a long time. If it has been, they may assume there is a problem with the property and will avoid it or make an offer below the asking price. Buyers also have the sales history available to them,

If the market changes after your property is listed, you may want to increase or decrease your price.

so they know if the price has increased or decreased. If it has decreased, they will want to know if there is a problem with the property or if the seller's circumstances have changed — for example, if the seller has already purchased another property.

Likewise, if the price has gone up, they want to know why it was increased. It is always a good idea to price your home at fair market value from the start, so buyers don't get suspicious. To avoid this problem, most agents would just cancel the listing and re-list the property again with a new price.

If you are working with an agent and you decide you want to reduce your price, you must give the agent authorization in writing, even if you have discussed a price reduction orally. Everything that pertains to real estate must be done in writing.

If you are selling your home on your own, without an agent, you should be aware that most FSBOs price their homes according to what they would like the property to sell for, rather than what the market is willing to pay. Be careful you don't fall into this trap. Have your house professionally appraised and ask a realistic price for it.

Pricing land only

If you are selling land only, without selling any improvements on the land, such as a house or a building, you will be pricing it against other land-only properties in the area. Depending on the land value, it is important to note that some financial institutions will require a larger down payment for purchasing land, and buyers may not always qualify for this type of financing.

Renovation value

Today's homeowners spend more than ever on renovations. Studies show that kitchens and bathrooms tend to top the list for remodelling. You should find out from your agent what improvements other than kitchen and bathroom renovations increase property value.

According to a RE/MAX survey, making your bathroom the best it can be will generate a 56 percent higher return on investment than the average popular renovation. The goal should be to create a spa-like environment in your bathroom by installing a soaker tub with relaxing jets, or perhaps a new steam shower stall. Kitchen upgrades deliver a 44 percent higher return on investment than the average, while repainting walls gives you a 29 percent better return, and installing or upgrading the fireplace in your home will generate an 11 percent greater return.

Some renovations that provide a negative return on investment are wall removal (-22 percent), having carpet instead of hardwood (-38 percent), installing a hot tub (-40 percent), and having a pool (-58 percent).

What If You Have a Mortgage?

If you are thinking of selling your home but you have not yet paid off your mortgage, you should discuss your situation with your realtor and your mortgage broker/lender. Ideally, the closing date for the sale of your current home will be ahead of the closing date for the purchase of your new home. That way, you can use the proceeds of the sale of your current home as a down payment on your new home.

If you decide to pay off your mortgage before the termination date, find out what the penalty will be.

You also want to arrange that the possession date of your new home is before the date you give possession of your current home to your buyer. Otherwise, you may not have a place to live for a few days.

You have a few options with your current mortgage. First, you can pay off your mortgage and get a new one for your new home. Second, you could take your mortgage to the new property. The third option is to have the seller assume your mortgage. Most mortgages are portable and assumable.

Getting a new mortgage

If you decide to pay off your current mortgage and get a completely new mortgage, you should know that lenders generally charge a pre-termination penalty if the mortgage is paid off before its expiry. The penalty charge is typically the higher of the interest-rate differential or three months' interest on fixed, closed mortgages.

The interest-rate differential is essentially the income the lender would have earned had you not pre-terminated the mortgage. Each lender has his or her own method for calculating this rate, but in general, the differential is the difference in interest rate between the contracted rate and the lender's rate for the remaining term of the mortgage.

A portable mortgage can be transferred from one property to another.

If, for example, there are two years left on the existing mortgage at 6 percent interest and the prevailing rate for a new mortgage is 4 percent, the lender will charge 2 percent (6 percent minus 4 percent) x amount of the mortgage x 2 years.

Some lenders will just charge a penalty of three months' interest, rather than the interest-rate differential, after the fifth year of the mortgage. This is for longer-term mortgages (i.e., those lasting seven to ten years).

On a variable rate mortgage, the penalty is usually three months' interest. However, there are lenders who charge less. Find out from your lending institution about rates.

Bridge loans

It is typical to sell your house first before buying your next home. This will remove unwanted stress as you try to juggle financing or face selling your home at a lower price. If, however, you are in a situation where you have to buy a new home before you sell the old one (e.g., if you are transferring to a new city and need a place to live), a bridge loan is a temporary loan that makes it possible for you to purchase your new home when that sale closes before the sale of your current home. Bridge financing allows you to borrow funds based on the net equity in the home you are selling.

Another reason for a bridge loan is if you were intending to use the proceeds from the sale of your current home for a down payment on your new home. In this instance you must ensure that the bridge loan is approved before the subject removal date. It is recommended that you discuss your situation with your mortgage broker/lender beforehand.

Ask your lender for detailed information on bridge loans, as lending institutions may stipulate minimum and maximum amounts for bridge loans, as well as terms ranging from 30 to 120 days.

Portable mortgage

Portable mortgages allow the homeowner to transfer his or her mortgage to a new property. By porting the mortgage, the homeowner saves prepayment penalties. In addition, there is an added benefit if the interest rate on the current mortgage is lower than the prevailing interest rate.

It is suggested that you check with your current lender about your mortgage's portability features. If your new purchase requires a higher mortgage amount, the lender may be able to blend the interest rate on your current mortgage with the prevailing interest rate on the additional amount you require. This makes sense if the interest rate on your current mortgage is lower than the prevailing interest rates. Some lenders can also extend the term of the mortgage.

Vendor take-back mortgage

A vendor take-back mortgage allows the seller to help a buyer purchase a property by loaning him or her a portion of the purchase price. Such a loan often comes with favourable or flexible terms, depending on the inclinations of the individual seller. The loan may be open, which means that the buyer can repay it at any time without penalty. The seller will negotiate the term of the loan with the buyer and may charge an interest rate lower than the prevailing market rate.

Another benefit is that it may help the buyer qualify for a mortgage.

Assumable mortgage

If you have a mortgage on a home you want to sell, it may be possible for a buyer to assume the mortgage on your current property. The buyer will continue to make monthly payments for the remaining term of the mortgage at the same interest rate you had. Buyers still need the lender's approval and will have to pass a credit check, just as they would if they applied for a new mortgage.

When interest rates are high, buyers may assume a mortgage that the seller obtained several years earlier, when interest rates were lower. This is a benefit to the buyer. By assuming the mortgage, buyers may also be helping the seller, because he or she can pass the mortgage along to the buyer instead of repaying the lender. Most lenders charge a penalty if a borrower repays a mortgage before its term expires. Some of the money that the seller saves by avoiding this penalty can be deducted from the price of the home.

COMPARATIVE MARKET ANALYSIS

COMPARATIVE MARKET ANALYSIS — HOUSE

Completed by (first and last name): _____

Employer: _____

Date house inspected: _____

Name of owner (first and last name): _____

Address: _____ City/Town: _____

Province: _____ Postal Code: _____

Information Section

Neighbourhood

Neighbourhood type:	Selling prices (past 3 months):	Current market:
❏ New	❏ Up	❏ Seller
❏ Improving	❏ Stable	❏ Buyer
❏ Stable	❏ Down	❏ Balanced
❏ Declining		

The typical marketing time is _____days to _____days.

The current number of competing houses for sale in the area: _____

House

Style of house: _____House age: _____years

Finish of exterior: _____

House size (square feet/metres): _____Size of lot: _____

Basement is: ❏ Full ❏ Partial

The garage has _____ space(s) for vehicle(s).

There are/is: ____ (number of) bedroom(s), ____ (number of) bathroom(s), and ____ (number of) fireplace(s).

Services:	**House is currently:**
❏ Municipal	❏ Occupied
❏ Well	❏ Rented
❏ Septic tank	❏ Vacant

Extras: _____

_____

Financial

First Mortgage: Second Mortgage:

Balance: $ _____   Balance: $ _____

Rate: _____   Rate: _____

Date due: _____   Date due: _____

Portable mortgage?   _____   Portable mortgage?   _____

Assumable mortgage?   _____   Assumable mortgage?   _____

Positive and Negative Marketing Features

P (Positive), N (Negative), or N/A (Not applicable)

_____ Property conforms to neighbourhood

_____ Quality of neighbourhood

_____ Plans for the future of the neighbourhood

_____ Topography

_____ Environmental issues (describe)_____

_____ Street (e.g., busy, quiet, etc.)_____

_____ Proximity to negative influences

_____ Builder reputation   _____ Construction quality   _____ Structural problems

_____ Lot

_____ Floor plan

_____ Internal condition   _____ External condition

_____ Cost to repair or renovate (approximate) $_____

_____ Other: _____

Recent Comparable Sales

Address 1

Address: _____Distance from subject: _____

Lot size: _____   House size: _____

Date sold:_____   Sale price: $ _____

The garage has _____space(s) for vehicle(s).

There are/is _____bedroom(s) and _____bathroom(s).

Features:_____

Circumstances: _____

Sample 5 — Continued

Address 2

Address: _____ Distance from subject: _____

Lot size: _____   House size: _____

Date sold: _____   Sale price: $ _____

The garage has _____ space(s) for vehicle(s).

There are/is _____ bedroom(s) and _____ bathroom(s).

Features: _____

Circumstances: _____

Current Competing Listings

Address 1

Address: _____ Distance from subject: _____

Lot size: _____   House size: _____

Date listed: _____   List price: $ _____

The garage has _____ space(s) for vehicle(s).

There are/is _____ bedroom(s) and _____ bathroom(s).

Features: _____

Circumstances: _____

Address 2

Address: _____ Distance from subject: _____

Lot size: _____   House size: _____

Date sold: _____   Sale price: $ _____

The garage has _____ space(s) for vehicle(s).

There are/is _____ bedroom(s) and _____ bathroom(s).

Features: _____

Circumstances: _____

Sale Price (Estimate)

Current and anticipated market condition for the area:

_____ Reasonable   OR   _____ Day selling period

In my opinion, the subject property should sell in the above-mentioned selling period within a range of $ _____ to $ _____, the midpoint of this range being $ _____.

Suggested List Price

I recommend an initial list price of $ _____ .

Recommendations for Marketing

_____

_____

_____
Signature

_____
Title

_____
Date

Comparative Market Analysis — Condominium

Basic Condo

Style of Condo Complex:

❏ Townhouse
❏ Semi
❏ Single
❏ rise building
❏ High-rise building

Other:_____

Number of Storeys: _____   Number of Units: _____

Complex age:_____ years

Size of units: from _____ to _____   Price range: from $_____ to $_____

Complex Occupancy:

_____% Owner occupied   _____% Rented   _____% Vacant

Interior condition of common elements: Exterior condition of common elements:

❏ Excellent   ❏ Excellent
❏ Good   ❏ Good
❏ Average   ❏ Average
❏ Fair   ❏ Fair
❏ Poor   ❏ Poor

Parking

Space:

- ❑ Excellent
- ❑ Not applicable
- ❑ Exclusive use
- ❑ Common use
- ❑ Owned
- ❑ Assigned

Monthly rental: $ _____

- ❑ Other: _____

_____

Type:

- ❑ Excellent
- ❑ Not applicable
- ❑ Underground garage
- ❑ Above ground with garage
- ❑ Above ground without garage
- ❑ Other: _____

Number of spaces: _____

Storage

Storage area: ❑ Yes   ❑ No

Size of storage area:_____ x_____

Locker space: ❑ Yes   ❑ No

Size of locker: _____ x _____

Number of lockers: _____

- ❑ Exclusive use
- ❑ Owned

- ❑ Common use
- ❑ Assigned   Monthly rental: $ _____

Financial and Legal

Monthly maintenance fees: $ _____

Comparable fees with other local condo complexes?   ❑ Yes   ❑ No

Fees include:

- ❑ Insurance
- ❑ Hydro
- ❑ Snow Removal
- ❑ Maintenance of common elements
- ❑ Other_____

_____

- ❑ Water
- ❑ Cable
- ❑ Garbage Collection

- ❑ Heat
- ❑ Internet
- ❑ Lawn Care/Landscaping

Sample 5 — Continued

Answer the following **yes** or **no**:

_____ Property conforms to neighbourhood

_____ Special assessment currently being levied

_____ Assessments pending or contemplated

_____ Property management company believes the reserve fund to be adequate
(The reserve fund currently contains $ _____.)

_____ Major repairs and/or improvements are currently underway

_____ Major repairs and/or improvements are pending

_____ Major repairs and/or improvements are being considered

_____ Outstanding and/or anticipated legal action(s)

_____ An independent reserve fund study has been completed
(Date of last reserve fund study: _____.)

Other factors that may impact subject's marketability:

_____

_____

_____

_____

_____

_____

_____

_____

PART 2

SHOULD I SELL MY OWN HOME OR GET HELP?

Chapter 6

SELLING ON YOUR OWN OR WITH A REAL ESTATE AGENT

After gathering data about your home, you should now decide if you are going to sell your home yourself, or if you are going to engage a partial-service or full-service realty company. You should consider the following factors when making this decision:

- Cost of selling the home
- Your personality and ability to do the job
- Pitfalls of selling without a real estate agent
- Services offered by agents
- Requirements for marketing the home (see Chapter 7)

A home that is being sold by the owner is called a FSBO (pronounced fizbo), which means "For Sale by Owner." A private sale is a specific kind of FSBO — it usually means a property is sold to a friend or relative of the owner, or to a friend of a friend by word of mouth, without the need for advertising.

What Are the Costs of Selling a Property?

As a seller, there are a variety of costs that you will incur whether you sell your home on your own or with an agent. These include the following costs:

Before deciding to sell your own home, assess your personality: Are you up for the task?

- Appraisal to determine your selling price
- Land title search
- Building inspector's fee for a pre-sale inspection
- Hiring a professional measurement company
- Marketing your home (e.g., print ads, flyers, websites, signage, distribution of print materials)
- Lawyer's or notary's fee to draw up the final paperwork
- Cost of paying off your mortgage before the agreed-on term ends

If you are selling your home on your own, all these costs will be an immediate out-of-pocket expense. If you are engaging the services of an agent, most of them will be covered by your agent and deducted from his or her commission after your home has been sold.

Do You Have What It Takes to Sell Your Own Home?

Many people have the "do-it-yourself" gene. They want to do as much as they can themselves without having to hire anyone, least of all a professional.

If you are one of these people, you should assess your characteristics and personality before deciding to sell your own home. You may want to ask yourself the following questions:

- Are you able to communicate effectively with potential buyers who have serious questions about your home?
- Can you accept feedback about your property, either positive or negative, without taking it personally?
- Will you be able to differentiate between bogus customers and bona fide buyers who are ready, willing, and able to purchase?
- Do you have the tenacity and perseverance it takes to sell a property?
- Are you outgoing and gregarious, or are you shy and easily intimidated?
- Can you adapt to a variety of different situations?

- Do you know enough contract law and real estate law to be aware of your legal responsibilities to the buyer so that you will minimize risks and potential liabilities and lawsuits?

In assessing your own personality, you need to admit your limits. If you realize you need help for some aspects of the sale, or if you are overwhelmed with the tasks that need to be done, hire someone to lend a hand or give you advice (e.g., a tax accountant, a real estate agent, a lawyer, etc.). Professionals are trained to perform a number of tasks and may have many years of experience that allow them to foresee problems that could arise. They know what extra steps to take to ensure that delays do not occur. They can usually put you in touch with other professionals who can give you help or advice in other areas of selling your home.

If you tend to be an introvert, buyers could misinterpret your body language and get the feeling that you are "weird" or untrustworthy. This is a major drawback for selling on your own, as it is crucial that buyers trust the seller and feel at ease with him or her. There have been several recent cases of tenants, or even people with no connection to a property, posing as a seller and persuading buyers to pay out thousands of dollars in deposit monies (sometimes cash). As a result, buyers tend to be on their guard and may not consider buying a house if they feel uncomfortable with the seller.

Even if you decide that you don't have the ability to sell your house on your own, there are many aspects of selling that most people can do, such as arranging viewings and hosting buyers at showings or open houses. If you decide that you can sell your house on your own, the legal aspects of real estate should always be dealt with by a professional — a lawyer or notary.

What Are the Pitfalls of Selling without an Agent?

If you want to sell your house on your own, you should be aware of the advantages and disadvantages of being a FSBO, and the public's perception of FSBOs.

The advantages are that you don't have to pay the real estate agent's commission, which can be a substantial saving, and you have the satisfaction of accomplishing a difficult task on your own

Buyers who look at homes for sale by owners may try to get you to lower the price because you don't have to pay a commission.

terms. According to a March 2003 report prepared by Star Inc. Research Consulting for the Canadian Real Estate Association (CREA), people who successfully sold their homes without the benefit of an agent appreciated that they had saved a lot of money, felt that they had more control in the process, and believed that they had maximized the value they received. One person said, "I sold my own home. It was great. I used a lawyer and a site called <salebyowners.com>. It cost me less than the commission. I scheduled my showings and I highly recommend it."

The disadvantages, according to a recent report from the National Association of REALTORS® in the US, are that FSBOs find the following tasks of a sale the most difficult (the percentage shows the number of people reporting each problem)*:

Getting the right price	19%
Understanding paperwork	30%
Preparing/fixing up home for sale	26%
Attracting potential buyers	7%
Having enough time to devote to all aspects of the sale	14%

FSBOs often tend to price according to what they would like their homes to sell for, rather than what the market is willing to pay. If you are selling your home on your own, make sure potential buyers know that you have priced your property according to fair market value. You may want to show them comparable listings in your neighbourhood.

Buyers who view FSBOs may be looking for a bargain and will try to get you to lower your price, arguing that you don't have to pay commission so you shouldn't be asking so much. One respondent in the 2003 Star Inc. report for CREA said, "People think that because you are not paying agent commissions, they should get a real big deal. And what they expect by way of a discounted price is more than the commission."

Real estate agents are subject to a code of ethics and are bound by Canadian laws to ensure a seller fully discloses a property's condition. As a result, if a seller does not engage an agent,

*Reprinted from "The 2004 National Association of REALTORS® Profile of Home Buyers and Sellers," ©2004 National Association of REALTORS®. Used with Permission. Reprinting, reproduction or transmission in any form (electronic media included) is prohibited without written permission. For more information, or to purchase a copy of the full report, call 1-800-874-6500.

buyers may question whether the seller is fully and honestly disclosing health problems, water damage, moisture ingress, and other problems. When buyers' agents see a property is a FSBO, they may shy away from it, believing it's too big a risk because the seller may not disclose the history and problems of the property, or what is disclosed may be inaccurate. Another comment in the 2003 Star Inc. report was: "We attempted to sell the house on our own. Agents called and said that they had an interested party but they would not bring the person unless we listed with someone. We had limited actual house viewings from just our ads."

One way to get around the reluctance of buyers' agents when you are selling your home on your own is to work with the agents and pay their commission in the event they produce a qualified, willing buyer to place an offer on your property. You would have to negotiate the fee with the buyer's agent and should take into account the following factors:

- The price that the buyer is willing to pay for your home
- The number of offers or requests for viewings you have had (i.e., if you've had no activity, you'll be more motivated to pay a commission)
- Your capital gain if, for example, you purchased the property at a low price and are now selling at a high price
- Your margins if you have not spent much on marketing

Often you will pay approximately half the regular commission, which is what the buyer's agent would get if your property were in an MLS listing. Other times, if the buyer's agent has had to do more than the usual work because you were late producing documents or didn't understand the legal complexities and the buyer's agent had to explain everything, he or she may want a full commission.

What Are the Benefits of Going with an Agent?

Two final comments from the Star Inc. report indicate why some people prefer selling (or buying) with an agent: "I think I can get a better price either way, buying or selling, with an agent. I think they are better able to look at the fine points and make sure that I am not missing anything" and "I like to think that if I use an agent, they are backed by a huge corporation. That means something to me. Maybe I am deluding myself, but at least I know where to find them if something goes wrong."

If your are selling your home on your own, you may want to work with buyers' agents — and pay them a commission.

These are two of the main reasons why people do contract with a real estate agent to sell their home. Agents have knowledge of the process and the market, so they are likely to get the best possible price for a property. They have a lot of experience dealing with people and situations and can act as a negotiator or mediator, bringing both parties to a mutual agreement. They can deal with the myriad marketing, legal, financial, and organizational details — with you helping as much or as little as you want. They can identify potential problems and help you avoid them, or they can deal with the problem before it becomes a major issue. And if things do go wrong, you can go to the real estate agency or the industry association to get satisfaction.

Agents also perform many duties "behind the scenes" that are not always apparent to the seller. They answer buyer and agent questions about the property or the seller, verify information the seller has provided, arrange appointments to view the home, and, after showing a home, will try to get some feedback, either from the buyers who view the property or their agents, about what they thought of the property, its condition, price, and so on. This information may help you make a better decision on price points.

Should you get a full-service agent or do you want to be involved?

If you are thinking of hiring an agent, you need to determine whether you will need full service, with every need being catered to and looked after by a single agent, or whether you prefer to be involved in the marketing and selling of your home. Sellers today can choose from full-service companies, partial-service companies, and "do-it-yourself" companies. Deciding on the best agency for you will depend on a number of factors, including the following:

- The amount of money you are willing to spend
- The amount of time you have to actively promote and market your property
- The amount of knowledge you have about real estate

Marketing and selling a home is a 24-hour-a-day, seven-day-a-week job. Most homes are not sold overnight, and it often takes weeks, even months, to sell a home. Most showings are done at a moment's notice and may occur during the daytime while you are at work, in the evenings while you are having dinner or relaxing, or on weekends when you want to be spending time with the family.

You may want to hand off this chore to an agent who knows how to deal with many types of people on a daily basis, from buyers, buyers' agents, home inspectors, mortgage brokers, and appraisers to lawyers or notaries. An agent also knows how to work with people to get the job done in a very limited time frame. (See Appendix 4 for more information about home and property inspectors.)

If you are interested in being involved — if you like meeting new people, perhaps, or have a flair for marketing or legal issues, or if you just want to save some money on fees and commissions — you may want to find an agent or company that welcomes active sellers. It is up to you to search for these companies in your local area and find out exactly which one suits your needs the best.

Some buyers prefer to deal with an agent whose name and reputation is well known.

Choosing the right agent for you

If you decide to go with an agent to sell your home, it is important to choose the right agent for you. You should go through an interview process so that you will know exactly what services each agent provides and what type of marketing tools he or she uses to sell your home.

It is also important to look at the agent's credentials, referrals, and testimonials, as well as to find out if the agent you are considering has faced a disciplinary hearing or if a complaint has been made against him or her. To get this information, you can call the real estate council of the province in which the agent is licensed. The council provides licences and training for real estate agents.

There are many ways to find an agent. Referral is one good source. Ask friends, family, neighbours, and colleagues who have recently sold a house if they would recommend their agent. You can also study print ads or websites, including <www.realtor.com> and <www.mls.ca>, which allow you to identify agents based on their location and specialties.

For some sellers, using a well-known name is important. Some buyers buy based on an agent's name or reputation. Many agents who have been in the industry for a long time have carved out a niche for themselves, specializing in a geographic area or demographic type. If you are selling a property suitable for such an agent's demographic or geographical specialty, you should consider using that agent. Other agents have a reputation for service and customer satisfaction. Perhaps there is an agent you or your family has worked with in the past. If you feel comfortable and familiar with that name, buyers might as well.

Some sellers find that working with a team of agents suits them well.

Equally important to some people is branding and company name recognition. The Canadian Real Estate Association defines "branding" as the proprietary visual, emotional, and cultural image that you associate with a company or product. When you think of Volvo, for example, you might think safety. The fact that you remember the brand name and have positive associations with that brand makes your product selection easier and enhances the value and satisfaction you get from the product. The same thing works for real estate agencies — you have a better feeling about some over others because of personal experience, stories you've heard from friends and colleagues, or even company advertising you've seen.

If you have a sense that buyers are drawn to a certain agent or agency due to personal or company name recognition, you might consider talking to that agent or agency about selling your house.

What about a team of agents?

You may choose to go with a team of agents instead of just one. The advantage of a team is that each person will have a specific role to play in the sale of your home. One may be in charge of listing the home, another will be responsible for showcasing your home before it is placed on the market, a third will be responsible for agents' open houses, and others will be in charge of print advertising (e.g., mail-outs, flyers, and advertisements), websites, and so on.

You should note that in this situation, not everyone in the team is a licensed agent. Some members may be licensed assistants or unlicensed assistants, which will limit their duties in terms of dealing with clients and contracts.

Find out what role each person plays in a team environment and inquire whether they are licensed or unlicensed assistants.

Types of listings

There are three basic types of real estate listings in Canadian markets: open, exclusive, and multiple listing service (MLS).

Open listing

This is a relatively loose, verbal agreement in which the seller gives one or more real estate agencies the authority to find a buyer for the property.

Exclusive listing

An exclusive listing gives one agent or agency the authority to offer a property for sale, lease, or exchange during a specific time period. The seller agrees to pay the listing agent a commission, even if the seller eventually sells the property himself or herself.

Multiple listing service (MLS)

A multiple listing service (MLS) is an exclusive listing with an added marketing feature. Multiple listing services are operated by local real estate boards. When you sign a multiple listing form, you authorize your agent to employ the services of co-operating agencies who are members of the real estate board.

Your property will be listed through MLS, reaching thousands of agents, and will be posted on the MLS website <www.mls.ca>, reaching the general public. This enables people to view your property and pertinent information, including photographs, 24 hours a day, seven days a week. You can even include a virtual tour of your property, with several pictures or videos showing 360-degree angles of each room.

If you choose to go with a multiple listing service, your property will get the widest market exposure.

The listing agreement

The relationship between a seller and an agent (the listing agent) is outlined in a contract, called a listing agreement, which ensures that both you and your agent have a complete understanding of your rights and responsibilities. Each of you will know what you can expect from the other and what is expected of you.

The listing agreement legally defines your arrangement with the agent and sets out in writing the following terms and conditions:

- The price you are asking for your home and your terms of sale
- The existing financing arrangements and whether this financing can be assumed by the new owner
- A list of items that are attached to the building (the "fixtures") that are not to be included in the sale (e.g., light fixtures, fireplace inserts, etc., are typically part of the sale price, so if there is a fireplace insert or crystal chandelier that you don't want to part with, you need to specify it). To avoid confusion or misunderstanding, you may want to take photographs of fixtures that are not to be included in the purchase price.

- The dates on which the contract begins and ends
- The date a new owner can take possession
- The commission the agent will receive once your home is sold

Before you sign a listing agreement, ensure that —

- everything has been filled out properly, and
- you understand all the terms in the contract.

Your agent should provide you with a copy of this agreement. Keep that copy in a safe, accessible place for future reference.

The listing agreement is a legal contract. You cannot simply terminate it without the consent of your agent. If your agent says that you can cancel the listing agreement at any time, ensure that you get this in writing. Sample 6 is an example of a listing agreement.

Responsibilities of listing agents

Once you have listed your property for sale, the listing agent has a legal duty to protect and promote your best interest at all times. He or she owes you — the principal — his or her undivided loyalty and must disclose to you any and all information obtained from any source that might influence your decision. The listing agent should not reveal any confidential information, which might jeopardize your bargaining position, to another person. The listing agent has a duty to exercise due care when answering questions and to treat all parties fairly and honestly.

Legal and professional requirements for agents

Most listing agents are members of the Canadian Real Estate Association (CREA), which is one of Canada's largest single-industry trade associations, representing approximately 66,000 real estate brokers/agents and salespeople working through 112 real estate boards, ten provincial associations, and one territorial association. CREA's primary mission is to represent its members at the federal level of government and to act as a watchdog on national legislation that pertains to the real estate industry. CREA has frequently taken strong stands to defend the public's right to own and enjoy property. (If you want to find out more about CREA and other real estate associations, there is contact information in Appendix 1.)

CREA members are governed by a professional code of ethics and standards of business practice. They are required to meet

Sample 6
LISTING AGREEMENT

LISTING AGREEMENT

Name of owner(s)/seller   Listing agent

BETWEEN: _____ AND _____

_____   _____

Address/Telephone number   Address/Telephone number

_____   _____

_____   _____

1. **Listing authority and term:**

    The Seller hereby lists exclusively with the Listing Agent the property described until
    11:59 p.m. on_____/_____/_____
                  month   day   year

2. **Property:**

    _____   _____
    Unit no.   Address of property

    _____   _____
    City/Town/Municipality   Postal Code

    Legal description:_____

    _____

    PID:_____

3. **Terms of sale:**

    _____   _____
    Listing price   Terms

4. **Listing agent's renumeration:**

    _____

    _____

5.   Co-operating agent's renumeration:

_____

_____

SIGNED, SEALED AND DELIVERED THIS _____ DAY OF _____ , 20—.

_____

Seller's signature

_____

Witness to seller's signature

_____

Seller's signature

_____

Witness to seller's signature

_____

Listing agent (print)

_____

Per: salesperson's signature

_____

Salesperson(s) (print)

financial and educational standards and to demonstrate integrity and character necessary to protect the public. Members support free and open competition, which means they decide for themselves the commission rates or fees they charge for services offered to the public, the division of those fees among co-operating members, and whether they work full time or part time, as part of an agency or on their own. The code of ethics encourages creative but honest advertising, and discourages members from filing complaints against competitors based on competition-related issues such as fee structure, comparative but truthful advertising, or acceptance of open or exclusive listings.

Like other professionals from dentists to lawyers, members of the real estate industry, including agents, home inspectors, mortgage brokers, appraisers, and lawyers/notaries, carry liability insurance. In the real estate industry this is called errors and omissions insurance. It protects the public in the event a real estate professional makes a mistake. If, for example, an agent without errors and omissions insurance were guilty of negligence, perhaps by not confirming that a property condition disclosure statement was filled out properly, the seller could be liable for some or all of the costs of the resulting damage to the buyer. Real estate is a very costly endeavour, and the awards given out by the courts can be in the hundreds of thousands of dollars, especially if the property involved is of significant value, so you should ensure that your agent has valid errors and omissions insurance.

Commission rates to agents vary. They often reflect the quality and quantity of service an agent provides.

The Agent's Commission

Agents work on a commission basis and receive payment only after the successful completion of a sale. The commission is usually stated as a percentage of the total sale price or as a fixed dollar amount. GST is charged on a commission.

The commission rate is not fixed by law or by any real estate board, and it varies from province to province. It must be negotiated between you and the agent you engage to help you. The commission rate often reflects the quality and quantity of service an agent provides. It is important that you, as a seller, do your due diligence and find out what type of service is best for you.

You should thoroughly discuss the commission before you sign a listing agreement. You and your agent should decide on the amount of compensation, the sources of payment, and the time or occasion on which the payment is to be made. All these details should be included in your listing agreement.

The listing agent traditionally shares his or her commission/fee with the agent working for the buyer. In the case of an MLS sale, your agent might also pay other brokers, agents, and salespeople who helped bring in a buyer. (The portion of commission shared in this instance is called a "commission split" and is often spelled out in the MLS information.)

Full commission on a quick sale

If your listing agent is able to sell your home in one day, you may still have to pay the full commission. Remember, there are many tasks that an agent does before the day your house goes on sale, and he or she may have already invested many hours for you, putting together an effective marketing plan. The agent may have spent money marketing your home by way of an Internet website, classified ads, direct mail ads, flyers, and open houses. Your agent's efforts should not go unnoticed or unpaid.

However, it is not uncommon for a listing agent to give a refund or some type of rebate for a quick sale. Some agents do this as a form of goodwill, but others don't. It basically depends on how much time and money your agent put into that "one day" sale.

How can you save on commission?

There are many ways you can pay less commission while making sure that your interests are protected at all times. You need to negotiate this with your agent *before* you sign a listing agreement. Many agents will reduce their commission if you take on some of their duties or pay some of the fees, which may include:

- Negotiate with the listing agent about how much he or she will spend on marketing. You can opt not to have some services performed (such as print advertising in the real estate newspapers or classified advertisements) or can agree to pay for them yourself.
- Offer to take on some of the responsibilities for showing the house. You can promise to be home to open the door for potential buyers and buyer's agents, or can have calls directed to you so you can make arrangements to show.

- You can also offer to be at the open house and perform some of the agent's duties, such as answering questions and providing accurate information about your property.

- Save the agent time and money by obtaining legal documents yourself. This can include the title search, Form "B" or estoppel certificate from the strata management corporation, strata council minutes and financial statements, and other documents named in Chapter 4.

- Tell the listing agent that you will use his or her services as a buyer's agent when looking for a home in exchange for a reduction in the commission rate.

If a property management company has been providing you with service that you are happy with, it's worth asking to see if the company has licensed real estate agents who will sell your home, providing you with some type of rebate or commission reduction.

Some developers offer incentives to agents who bring buyers to their projects.

Bonuses and other incentives for agents

Agents work on a commission, so it is important to motivate them to bring in buyers to look at your property. It is not uncommon for homeowners and developers to provide bonuses or other incentives for agents. Developers provide bonuses, leases on expensive automobiles, trips, and other incentives to agents who bring in buyers to purchase their projects.

Sellers might offer a bonus to their listing agent if they are anxious to sell because they have already bought another house, they have been relocated and are leaving town soon, they are selling because of a divorce or a death, etc.

You could offer a bonus to buyers' agents for these reasons as well. You can include this bonus as part of your marketing costs — and you should include information about it in your advertising.

What Is the MLS System and What Can It Do for Sellers?

As mentioned earlier, the multiple listing service (MLS) is a marketing feature operated by local real estate boards. A property listed through MLS will reach thousands of agents and will be posted on the MLS website, reaching the general public. All agents who are members of the local real estate board can list properties through MLS.

An MLS feature sheet contains an in-depth description of your property, including the following elements and more:

- All features of your home, from bedrooms to sundecks
- Total living area
- Frontage and depth
- Size of lot
- Dimensions of property
- Previous year's taxes
- Monthly maintenance fees
- Distance to schools
- Distance to transportation
- Agent's remarks
- Price

The MLS feature sheet is an important document because potential buyers rely on the accuracy of the information in it. The information is included in a computerized database for the real estate board in your area. Agents can obtain a list of properties for sale from the local board or by browsing <www.mls.ca> or <www.realtylink.org>.

The MLS system provides information about your property to other boards, in other cities, regions, and countries. If you think about the numbers of investors and potential home-buyers in your city and province, and then consider the number of people who might be thinking of moving there from other provinces and even other countries, it becomes clear that the MLS system is a great marketing and selling tool.

In addition to the MLS websites, agents also have access to regularly updated catalogues of MLS listings, which allow them to give clients without web access a look at properties in the area they are considering.

PART 3

HOW DO I GO FROM MARKETING TO COMPLETING THE SALE?

Chapter 7
MARKETING YOUR HOME

After gathering the data about your home, deciding on a price, and deciding on a budget, you (if you're selling on your own) or your agent will prepare a marketing plan, with brochures or flyers, advertising, website, a feature sheet, and a schedule of open houses.

What Do You Do to Market a Property?

Once you have determined the selling points of your home and the target market (see Chapters 1 and 2), you need to set up a marketing plan and decide how much you will spend on marketing costs. There are a variety of methods for letting people know your home is for sale, and you can use some or all of the following methods:

- Classified ads in newspapers or real estate papers
- Display advertisements in newspapers or real estate papers
- Flyers to be delivered in a targeted neighbourhood or posted where your target market will see it (i.e., for young families, post at a daycare or rec centre; for professionals, at a downtown coffee shop)
- Information sheets that are distributed to prospective buyers visiting the home

Spending money on advertising is a crucial part of a sales strategy.

- Website with pictures, floor plans, and other information about the home
- Open houses (see Chapter 8)

Print advertising and websites

If you are a FSBO doing print advertising (classified or display ads), take some time to look at similar ads that are already running. This will give you an idea of what information you should include and how you should set up your ad. If you are including a picture in a display ad, make sure that it is a good quality photo and will reproduce well in the newspaper. You may need to hire a designer to put the ad together. The same goes for flyers and information sheets. You want to present a professional image to potential buyers. Unless you have website production skills, you should probably hire an experienced computer firm to put together a website if you want to advertise your home on the Internet.

The following websites will allow FSBOs to post information, contact numbers, and photos of their property for a small price:

- www.forsalebyowner.com
- www.fsbo.ca
- www.homesellcanada.com

If you are selling on your own, you will pay for marketing up front and will either spend time producing ads and websites yourself or will pay for someone to do it. Though you may not want to spend money on advertising, such expenditures are a crucial part of the home-selling process unless you can arrange a private sale by word of mouth.

If you hire a real estate agent, he or she will incur some of these costs as part of a marketing plan and will deduct the costs from the commission after your property is sold. Ask your agent to itemize exactly which costs are included and which are not. The type and amount of advertising an agent does depends on the type of real estate market that exists at the time you are selling. Some agents spend up to 25 percent of their commission on marketing and "farm advertising," in which print advertising (e.g., flyers, mail-outs, newsletters, and Just Listed cards) featuring your home is sent out to a specific neighbourhood.

Most agents today also produce an Internet marketing plan to showcase and market your property around the world. Someone relocating from the United States, Asia, or Europe, for example, can view your property from the comfort of their home, 24 hours a day, seven days a week. This may include a virtual tour of your property.

Signage and tools of the trade

If you are selling your home on your own, you will incur costs to purchase "tools of the trade." For example, For Sale signs with your phone number. If your property is not on a busy street, you may want to put up directional arrows to show where the house is located. You could put up balloons, flags, colourful banners, or similar paraphernalia to draw attention to your property, just as agents do when they are advertising an open house.

There may be restrictions on the type, number, or placement of signs, so check your community's zoning by-laws for a provision limiting the use of outdoor and indoor advertisements and other graphic displays. Traditionally, sign restrictions for real estate agencies relate to office signs, such as billboard advertising. However, many municipalities throughout Canada have instituted sign restrictions regarding For Sale and Open House signs that limit both the size and number. For example, some municipalities restrict the use of directional signs at main intersections as they are a distraction — especially in high traffic areas or in areas that may restrict visibility. Even rural municipalities have such restrictions, so it is a good idea to do some research before investing in signage.

Other tools of the trade you might want to invest in while selling your home are a cell phone, a digital camera, a website, and business cards with contact numbers.

Marketing to friends, relatives, and neighbours

Make sure you let friends, relatives, and neighbours know you intend to sell. In many cases, especially when selling condominiums, tenants or homeowners in the building may have friends or relatives who want to purchase a unit in the same development.

If you end up selling privately, with no real estate agent involved, it is a good idea for both you and the buyer to obtain legal representation to draw up the contract of purchase and the final bill of sale, and to ensure that the title is clear. If you find a buyer for your property after you've hired an agent, you may still be required to pay the agent's fees.

Always use action words, such as, "Call today!" "Don't delay!" "Make an appointment!"

Advertising

Whether you are creating print advertisements, classified advertisements, brochures, and websites for a FSBO or to reduce the commission you pay an agent, here are some marketing dos and don'ts to remember:

- Newspaper advertising should be brief, but to the point. Remember that each line of print costs you money, so use it well. Price and location are important, as are the number of bedrooms and bathrooms, and, if you have room, the square footage of living area and lot size for detached houses.

- Don't include the street address in your advertisement, just a phone number to call. This will prevent people coming by at all hours to view the property. FSBOs need to be sure that people viewing their home are serious about buying, so it's a good precaution to try and get a sense of a person over the phone, judging his or her voice, manner, attitude, questions, and so on. Not including your address in the ad will also protect you from potential robbers.

- If there are restrictions, such as no pets or no rentals, indicate this in order to eliminate some calls.

- Be creative in your advertisement, but don't embellish. Use descriptive words that will target your market — "private patio" or "low maintenance." Always use action words, such as, "Call today!" "Don't delay!" "Make an appointment!" "Be the first to see it!" Action words help potential buyers feel emotionally involved. Avoid words that may be offensive or childish.

- Make sure that your telephone numbers are correct. You should include work numbers and cell phone numbers if you have them; real estate is a 24/7 job, and buyers or their agents need information right away. If they have to leave a message on voice mail or with an answering service, they may not wait for the answer. (Don't forget, if you have to be away from home or work, to forward calls to whoever is helping you sell your home.)

- A picture is worth a thousand words. For brochures or feature sheets, make sure that you have a clear photo of the front of your home. Avoid taking photos at night or on a cloudy, rainy day. Equally important are multi-photo "tours" of your home that include shots of the interior and exterior. If you have a waterfront, lake, or city view, be sure to show it to potential buyers. (For security reasons, do not leave out precious items, family heirlooms, jewellery, art work, and so on, when you take photos. Thieves sometimes check out photos of houses on sale to see if there is anything worth stealing.)

When describing your home, use words and features that are enticing.

- When describing your home, use words and features that are enticing. An example of a brochure or website text would be:

> *Quiet, spacious, top-floor corner penthouse suite. Bright, 2 large bedrooms, 2 bath condo in Fairview with view of downtown. Quiet courtyard side of the building. Gourmet kitchen with stainless steel appliances, hardwood flooring, gas fireplace, walk-in closet, and many other quality finishings throughout. Shocking value! Professionally renovated! Just steps to the seawall and Granville Island. Private entrance on ground level with south-facing balcony. Pet friendly and rentals allowed. Bonus: 2 parking stalls.*

- Be honest in your print advertising. Exaggerations and misrepresentations will not only result in lost sales, but will lead you into trouble. If, for example, you say in your ad "Unit has 5 appliances," but then you decide you don't want to sell the appliances, the buyer can go back to the ad to prove that the appliances are part of the purchase price and must stay with the unit. Don't describe a home as "solid," when it is actually a tear-down, or claim a property has hardwood floors when they are just plywood or laminate. Don't include "water view" as a feature in your listing, when you have to stand on tiptoes and crane your neck to catch a glimpse of the water!

For agents, misleading advertising reflects poorly on the industry. If it violates CREA's code of ethics and standards of business practice, the agent may face discipline by his or her board or association. Misleading advertising is also a criminal offence, and agents or individuals who produce misleading ads can be sued by the buyer on the grounds of misrepresentation. The general prohibition against misleading advertising applies to both the literal wording and the general impression created by an advertisement to determine if the ad is misleading in a material respect.

Chapter 8
SHOWING YOUR HOME

Once you've started advertising your house, you will get calls from buyers and buyers' agents to view it. You will also want to host open houses for the general public or agent tours. To prepare for these, you need to look at your home and fix everything from the exterior to the interior, including garages or carports, storage and locker areas, crawl spaces, basements, and attics. It is important to remove unwanted clutter in order to show your home to its best advantage. Also, make sure you keep valuables out of sight when your house is being shown so they are not a lure for thieves.

If you are using an agent, his or her most complex job may be arranging for potential buyers to view the property. If you are living in the home, or if you have tenants living there, the agent must make sure that the house is available for viewing when he or she has made appointments. Some agents will indicate certain viewing times in their ads. For example, they might say houses are available for viewing on weekdays only or weekends only, or they may be even more specific, giving particular days or times (i.e., from 1 p.m. to 5 p.m. on Monday and Wednesday, or weekends only from 5 p.m. to 8 p.m.). Otherwise, the agent will check with you before finalizing a viewing. This is very important if there are older people or young children living in the house, or guests, as certain times may be more convenient than others for the sellers.

For your own safety, make appointments with people to show your home — don't allow stangers to walk in whenever they choose.

It is important to note that there may be requests for showing with very little notice. For example, if a buyer is in town for a day and would like to see a few properties, if yours in the only one available to view on short notice, the buyer may just choose to purchase your property.

If you have tenants, you need to make sure that you are giving enough notice before a viewing, as stipulated by the provincial ministry of housing (see section on "Showing a Rental Property").

Even if your property is vacant, it's always good for the agent to let you know when he or she has arranged a viewing — just in case you are letting someone stay in the house or apartment and have forgotten to notify the agent.

If you are selling on your own, you will have to keep track of these details yourself and be prepared to show your house at all hours of the day, including statutory holidays and long weekends.

Protecting Yourself and Your Family

When dealing with the public, you need to be careful not to put yourself in harm's way. You are vulnerable at open houses and even more so when meeting a complete stranger for an appointment to view a vacant property. Agents often double up when they are hosting an open house or showing a property, and this is good advice for FSBOs as well. Have a friend or your spouse accompany you. Make sure that someone knows of your whereabouts at all times. Carry a cell phone with preset emergency numbers, establish a distress code with family members, and do not include the word "vacant" in your advertisement.

If you have elderly people or children in your home, it's important to focus on making sure that they are always safe and that strangers can't come in at whatever time suits them. This is another reason not to include your address in advertising. It's best to have people phone you so that you can set the time they will visit your property.

Showcasing Made Simple

Statistics tell us that 95 percent of buyers purchase on emotion. Buyers need to absolutely *love* your home if they are going to purchase it. To capture the attention of buyers, some agents hire an interior designer to help prepare a home so it achieves its maximum selling potential. Often designers will move, or remove, furniture in your home to highlight certain features or functionality. Some agents have used home stagers or set designers to prepare homes for show.

Home staging companies offer services that range from simply organizing the home so it is free of clutter or adding touches such as dramatic lighting, luxurious throw pillows on a sofa, and Art Nouveau on the walls, to removing all the furniture from the home and storing it for a few days or replacing furniture with rented furniture. The aim is always to earn a higher price and faster sale. Your real estate agent can recommend a home stager in your area, or check the Yellow Pages or the Internet.

When developers or real estate agents are selling a new development, they will involve architects, designers, and interior decorators to make the most of their show homes and demonstrate their highest potential. Such properties are enhanced with the latest in light fixtures, colour and design trends, and so on. These homes can give you ideas and inspiration on how to show your own home.

If you are going to prepare your house on your own, here are a few tips:

- The environment should be generic and neutral, with no personal effects that buyers might find objectionable or questionable. Your home should be a white canvas in which the placement of each piece of furniture, painting, or decoration has been meticulously thought out to highlight the best of the property.

- The colours and interior decorating should emphasize the home's unique features and functionality. Many people have their own design and decorating ideas, which may not always appeal to buyers. It's best to use colours that are muted or in keeping with the latest trends.

- You want the house to smell new and clean. Adding a fresh coat of paint will appeal to buyers and give them the sense of being in a new home. Get rid of any smells from pets, food, tobacco, cooking oil, or gas. Sweeten your home with baking soda or air fresheners.

- Be sure to shut every window so that no noise penetrates the home. If it is a new development, chances are there are double- or triple-glazed windows and sound barriers, so that

If you are selling a rental property, you must give the tenant advance notice for showing the property.

the house is quiet, even if it is on a busy street. You can further enhance the atmosphere by playing tranquil music.

Showing a Rental Property

If you are using an agent to sell a rental property that is vacant, typically he or she will use a lock box to access the unit. A lock box is a computerized system that provides the keys to the apartment and unit only to qualified agents who have obtained the box's security access code from the listing agent. In the event that the unit or property is vandalized, or if objects have gone missing, the computerized system lets you know which agent has used the lock box.

The general public has no access to this lock box, so you may want to either ask a trusted neighbour in the building to help you with the showings, or give a friend, neighbour, or relative a spare set of keys so that they can show the property if you're not available. There is also a keypad security system on the market that you can buy and install at your home. You or another person showing your home can punch a code into the keypad that is attached to the door. Punching in the access code unlocks the door without the use of keys.

If there is a tenant in the apartment or property that you are selling, you must comply with the Residential Tenancy Act (RTA) of your province. The RTA generally contains provisions that affect both the ending of a tenancy for landlord use of the property (e.g., a sale) and the showing of a rental property. In British Columbia, for example, a landlord must give the tenant written notice that he or she will be accessing the property. The notice must be given within a certain period before entry (usually at least 24 hours, and not more than 30 days, before the entry) and should include the following information:

- The purpose for entering, which must be reasonable
- The date(s) and time(s) of entry, which must be between 8 a.m. and 9 p.m. unless the tenant otherwise agrees

A landlord can give notice setting out a reasonable schedule of viewing times for an upcoming period. However, the RTA also sets out a tenant's rights to reasonable privacy and freedom from unreasonable disturbance. For more information, check the RTA for your province or territory. See Appendix 3 for a list of housing ministries across Canada.

Showing a Vacation Home

If you are selling a vacation home that is far from your home community, you should consider all your options for selling the property in the most efficient way (and avoiding the time and money involved in commuting back and forth to the vacation home). You may want to consider the following options:

- You can provide keys to the potential buyer if you are not worried about giving a stranger access to your home and property. In this situation you need to assess the risk to you and decide if the person is a bona fide buyer.

- Alternatively, you can provide keys to the potential buyer after obtaining a security deposit — perhaps a credit card number, a certified cheque, or something of that nature.

- You could leave your keys with a trusted friend or neighbour who lives near the vacation property and who is willing to show the home to potential buyers.

- You may want to hire a real estate agent in the area to sell your home. Most agents do not go out of their specific geographical area, but are very knowledgeable about their own locale, so obtaining an agent in that area can be the best way to sell a vacation property.

Open Houses and Agent Tours

As part of your marketing strategy, you should host a public open house to showcase your home to potential buyers and to agents. If you are using a real estate agent, he or she will likely arrange an open house specifically for agents during the first week or so that the house is listed. This event will be on a weekday, and all agents who are members of the local real estate board will be invited. Buyers may attend as well if they are available, but most buyers attend open houses on weekends.

If you are selling your house on your own, it is difficult to let all the local agents know about your open house in a cost-effective way. Even using your time to e-mail agents in your area about the open house may not be fruitful. The best option may be to contact the top ten agents in your area to see if they have any clients who may be interested.

It is important to know the dos and don'ts of showcasing and showing your home to potential buyers and agents. The following

Use attention-grabbing signage to advertise your open house.

are some tips for showing your home, either at an open house or for a private viewing:

Dos

1. Do be professional at all times. Greet each person who comes in, and wear appropriate attire. You want to look professional but also approachable, so good-quality casual clothes are okay, but not sweats, shorts, or grubby T-shirts.

2. Do ask visitors to sign a guest book so that you will know who has attended.

3. Do make sure that you have all the data in your feature sheet correct. Buyers rely on the accuracy of the information provided, such as the total square footage, size and measurements of the living area, and so on.

4. Do make sure that you have plenty of feature sheets to hand out.

5. Do have the lights on. Even if it is daytime, leave the lights on so that people can see everything.

6. Do ask a friend, relative, or neighbour to open the door for buyers and agents should you be late for an open house. Do not be late for a private showing. Make sure that you leave ample time to open your house. Most buyers' agents have tours scheduled and show homes one after the other. If you are late, chances are the buyers will not wait and will move on to the next home.

7. Do make the beds, tidy up the insides of closets, clean bathrooms, remove all garbage, and leave the lights on. You could also turn on the fireplace, turn on the music, and light some candles for ambiance.

8. Do provide a contact name and number where you can be reached at any time of the day and night and on weekends.

9. Do put a sign out for your open house before and during the event. Signage is an important tool in the real estate industry. Place a sign at your house and directional signs on the main streets. Attach balloons, flags, and other attention-grabbing items to your house and the sign in front of it.

10. Do bake muffins! Studies have shown that the smell of goods baking in the oven stimulates the senses and gives the feeling of being "at home."

11. Do ask agents to leave their business cards behind. It is always important to find out who has come into your home, and you may want to take the opportunity, especially if you are selling your home on your own, to call the agents back to find out if their client liked the home and if they could provide any feedback about the home — for example, if it is priced fairly.

12. Do have open houses on weekends and at times when there are other open houses in your area. Usually this is afternoons between 1 p.m. and 3 p.m. during the fall and winter, and from 2 p.m. to 4 p.m. during spring and summer.

13. Do open your storage lockers, sheds, and basements to show potential buyers all the storage area that is available to them.

14. Do make sure that you provide buyers and their agents with room to park. If parking is too difficult, buyers may get frustrated and move on to the next property. Instead, provide buyers with directional signs indicating where to park.

Don'ts

1. Don't have a showing during or around mealtime. Some foods may be fragrant to some, yet offensive to others.

2. Don't be around if you have a hard time accepting negative comments about your taste in décor (or lack thereof). If you are selling with an agent, you can have him or her host the open house. If it is a FSBO, ask a trusted friend or relative to be the host.

3. Don't have young children or elderly people at the house during a showing. Potential buyers want to feel free to move about the home without intruding on other people's spaces.

4. Don't lie about something important to the buyers. If you don't know the answer, ask them to leave their name and phone number so you can get in touch with them after you find the answer to their question.

5. Don't be shy. If buyers come into your open house with food or candy, smoking cigarettes, or wearing muddy shoes, ask them politely to remove their shoes or refrain from eating or smoking until after they leave.

Don't leave valuables lying around your home when you are hosting an open house.

6. Don't have pets around — barking dogs can scare potential buyers away, and cats may set off allergies. Have someone take your pets away while you are showing your home, or leave your dog in its kennel.

7. Don't be alone! Make sure that you have friends or family members working alongside you so that you can make the most of an open house. If you are showing a condominium, for example, you may want to escort potential buyers around to see the parking spaces, storage lockers, common areas, and other amenities of the building, yet still bring people into the building and unit at the same time. If you are showing a condominium, the strata corporation may insist, for the safety and security of other homeowners, that you escort all visitors and guests in and out of the building. You would need more than one person helping you to do this.

8. Don't sit down! Make sure that you are always showing guests around the property — after all, open houses don't last very long!

9. If you notice suspicious behaviour, whatever it is, pay attention to your gut feeling. Make sure you don't turn your back on these strangers or let them browse through the rooms on their own. If you feel very uncomfortable, there is nothing to prevent your refusing to allow someone to enter your home.

10. Don't leave out sharp objects — knives on the counter, for instance — or anything else that could harm people viewing your house. Make sure that you make your home as safe as possible.

11. Don't leave valuables — coin and stamp collections, jewellery, loose money, keys, remote controls, or anything that can be carried away quickly — lying around your home. Some buyers are actually thieves and are there to steal from you. Ask people with knapsacks to leave their bags in the front foyer.

12. Don't have an all-day open house. Have your house open for two or three hours during the time when the general public is out looking.

Chapter 9
THE OFFER

As you show your home at an open house or privately, the buyers' body language will give you a hint whether the buyers like your property or not. One of the telltale signs of approval is a buyer smiling and nodding his or her head while you are talking about the features of the home. Another sign is a buyer asking a lot of questions about the property. It means the buyer is trying to obtain as much information as possible about the home so that in the event he or she makes an offer, it is based on facts rather than just emotion.

Some buyers take photographs when on a tour, but they generally take photos only of the homes that have potential — homes they are considering purchasing. Therefore, if you see buyers with their cameras out, you will know that they are interested in your property.

Buyers who take their time going over the property, carefully examining bedrooms, bathrooms, and closet space, are also sending a signal that they are interested in your property — especially when they envision their furniture in your home. Statements like "This could be Jane's room" or "Our armoire will go perfectly here" suggest that the buyers are interested.

Finally, buyers who request a second or third showing or buyers who physically measure room sizes, especially when they bring along a friend or family member, are definitely interested in the property. Often buyers have already made up their mind, but they need a second opinion to help them in their decision-making process by pointing out possible problems they have overlooked or by confirming their positive feelings. This is especially true for a buyer purchasing alone.

The Buyer

Today's buyers are more educated about the buying process and are therefore more proactive and in control. Statistics show that more than 75 percent of buyers go online first to research the buying process, look for properties, search for a qualified real estate agent, and so on.

Buyers want assurances that their interests are protected at all times. Because of this, you will find many buyers engaging a buyer's agent to represent them or a lawyer to help them with the transaction. Further, buyers who have seen friends and family facing financial hardships after purchasing real estate want to be careful before they purchase. Buyers are aware of their legal rights and responsibilities and will seek out their own professionals — such as building inspectors, surveyors, and so on — to ensure that their legal interests are protected.

Buyers' biggest hurdles are fear of writing the contract, fear of not having enough money for a down payment, and fear of rejection. They might also fear they are paying too much, that the owner may not have the right to sell the property, or that something is wrong with the property or will go wrong with it and they'll be stuck with no recourse. There are instances when buyers purchase and then realize that the seller is moving to another city or country. This can cause buyers concern, as it will be more difficult to seek damages should problems arise.

Separating qualified buyers from the lookers

As a seller, you will also want assurances that your interests are protected and that potential buyers are capable of paying what they offer for your property. Especially if you are selling your home on your own, it is difficult to distinguish qualified, willing buyers from people who are just curious neighbours. Some buyers say that they have financing in place even when they don't.

Most buyers' agents today will pre-screen their clients to determine their capacity before taking them out on tours to view properties. Buyer qualification is the process of uncovering a buyer's motivation, needs, desires, and ability to pay, although it is not always an exact method of determining a client's capacity or ability to obtain financing. Some buyers' agents will ask all potential clients for a copy of a letter of commitment from the buyer's financial institution. This will show exactly how much mortgage financing the person is pre-qualified for and how much purchasing power they have. It will also show the agent that the client has taken the time to go through the pre-qualification process. If you are selling on your own, you can ask a potential buyer for a letter of commitment to ensure he or she can obtain the financing for a home purchase.

An offer from a buyer must be in writing to be valid.

Who can be legally bound by a contract?

It is important to note that to be legally bound to a contract, the parties entering into the agreement must be legally competent. Infants or minors, mentally incapacitated persons, and intoxicated persons are protected by law so that others will not take advantage of them. The age of majority differs in each province. In Alberta, Saskatchewan, Manitoba, Ontario, Quebec, and Prince Edward Island, the age of majority is 18. In British Columbia, New Brunswick, Nova Scotia, Newfoundland, Nunavut, Northwest Territories, and Yukon, it is 19.

When You Receive an Offer

In real estate, everything must be in writing, so if someone verbally offers to buy your house, you don't actually have an offer until the buyer has written it down in a contract of purchase and sale.

When you, as a seller, receive an offer from a buyer, there are several things you should look at to evaluate the validity of the offer. These include the condition precedents or subject clauses (including time clauses and financing clauses), the buyer's letter of commitment, and the amount of deposit being offered.

Condition precedents

On any offer presented to you, there will be condition precedents or subject clauses. These outline conditions that must be met before the agreement to purchase is finalized. Some of the most common condition precedents are the following items:

- The buyer will purchase the property on the condition that he or she is able to find a lender who will finance the deal.
- The buyer will purchase if he or she is satisfied with the building inspection report and the title search.
- For a strata title, a buyer may want to see two years' worth of minutes, financial statements, rules, and by-laws of the strata corporation, a Form "B" or estoppel certificate (showing there are sufficient monies in the contingency fund), an engineer's report, and a strata plan.

When going through the offer, if you are uncertain about any of these condition precedents, seek legal advice immediately. If you accept the offer and sign it, you have accepted the terms and conditions in the contract.

Time clauses

All contracts — whether a listing agent contract, a buyer's agent contract, a contract of purchase and sale, or an offer to purchase — have a time clause, which sets out when the contract is in effect and when it ends. In the case of an offer, the buyer puts in a time clause that says how long the offer is open for acceptance. The seller is given perhaps 24 to 48 hours to respond. (In a hot market, this may sometimes be shorter.)

Similarly, there is also a time limit for removing condition precedents. This may be one or two days or one or two weeks. It typically depends on how active the market is. The important thing to remember is that both parties — the buyer and the seller — have to be in agreement for the time clause to take effect. In the event that not all condition precedents can be removed within the time frame given — for whatever reason — the seller and the buyer both have to agree to an extension. This should be outlined in an addendum, with both parties signing off on it to indicate their agreement.

Financing

There are three commonly used methods of paying for real estate:

- New first mortgage
- All cash

- Assumption of an existing mortgage

If a buyer offers you an "all cash" transaction, seek the advice of your lawyer or real estate agent immediately. This may be an offer in which the buyer is either not making the purchase of your property subject to obtaining a mortgage or the buyer may be confident that she or he can obtain financing. If the buyer does not have the full payment in cash or cannot obtain financing by the closing date, the seller may seek legal action.

You should look at the financing clause carefully to see what type of down payment the buyer is making. If the buyer is offering a 25 percent to 30 percent down payment, it is probably unlikely that he or she will have difficulty obtaining financing. However, if the buyer is offering a zero down payment (which means the buyer does not have any money saved for the purchase) or a high-ratio loan, this transaction may be a higher risk for both the seller and the bank.

For the seller, it may mean that the buyer will be unable to remove the condition precedent of financing and the deal may not go through. In such a case, you may not want to give the buyer much time for removing condition precedents, as you don't want your property tied up for a week or ten days while the buyer tries to get financing.

Alternatively, you can ask the buyer for a copy of the mortgage pre-approval. If you are still not satisfied, you may want to get permission from the buyer to talk to her or his broker/lender to find out more about the buyer's ability to obtain the necessary financing.

Check the amount of deposit, or stakeholder, that the buyer is offering you. The higher the deposit or stakeholder, the lower the chance of that buyer walking away from the offer. Any deposit or stakeholder monies must be deposited in a lawyer's or real estate agent's trust account. See the section on "Deposits and down payments" below.

The higher the deposit a buyer offers, the lower the chance of that buyer walking away from the offer.

When You Receive Multiple Offers, Low-ball Offers, or Agent Offers

You may also have to deal with competing or multiple offers, identical offers, low-ball offers, or offers from salespeople, all of which bring up different issues.

Make sure you understand the
rules for accepting back-up
offers.

Competing offers, multiple offers, and back-up offers

In a seller's market, or if your property is unique or priced well, it is not uncommon to receive more than one offer. When you have two offers for your property, they are called competing offers. When there are more than two offers, you have a multiple-offer situation. Look carefully at the price, terms, conditions, financing, and, in particular, dates of completion and possession set out in each offer.

Procedures governing multiple-offer presentation vary by provincial jurisdiction and/or real estate agency. Agents or lawyers should fully explain such procedures, along with the risks and benefits, to their clients when entering into an agency relationship. FSBOS should contact a lawyer or the law association of their province to find out what rules apply where they live. Make sure that you understand how each offer comes into effect, especially if you accept one offer and then accept another offer as a back-up.

For sellers, multiple offers present both an opportunity and a risk. They present an opportunity because you can choose the offer that is best for you (i.e., highest price, fewest condition precedents; earliest possession date) rather than having only one offer that may not be ideal. They can be a risk because you might get carried away and counter more than one offer at a time. If more than one buyer accepts your counter-offer, you would then have to proceed with two or more closings, and as you are only able to sell your property once, the unsuccessful buyers would likely sue you for damages.

The best approach is to openly and fully discuss all options, benefits, and drawbacks with a qualified professional. If there is an agent and real estate agency involved, fully discuss their policies regarding multiple offers and the sequencing of offer presentations. If you are selling on your own, talk to a lawyer.

Identical or nearly identical offers

No two offers are identical. They may be identical in price, but there will be other terms and conditions that make each buyer's situation unique. For example, one offer may have few or no conditions (i.e., clauses saying the sale is conditional on some other action or event, such as the buyer obtaining financing or the property passing a building inspection).

Look at each buyer's financial capabilities, financing, dates for completion and possession, and so on. If you can, meet with the buyers. You can probably get a good sense of their financial capabilities by asking for their financial information up front, before accepting their offer.

You can choose one buyer over the other according to your personal preference. Perhaps you want to see your home sold to a family rather than a developer, or vice versa. Maybe you're in a hurry to sell, and one buyer offers an earlier completion and possession date.

Low-ball offers

If you are selling your home on your own, don't be surprised when you receive low-ball offers. Many buyers, when they see a property is a FSBO, tend to make an offer well below the seller's asking price, thinking that it may be accepted.

Sometimes buyers' agents will ask you or your agent why you are selling. If the buyer's agent believes you are highly motivated to sell, he or she might think that a lower offer will be accepted. If you are dealing with an agent and are not motivated to sell unless you get your full price, you should tell your agent to state that the seller wants only full price. Otherwise, it is a waste of everyone's time to have offers presented for less than the full price. If you are selling on your own, you can state in ads and information sheets that the price is firm, that there will be no negotiation, and that you want nothing less than the full price.

Offers from salespeople to purchase for themselves

If listing agents decide to acquire real estate for themselves, they must take extreme care to ensure that their duty is not put into conflict with their interest as a principal in the transaction. They should disclose to the seller what they plan to do with the property (i.e., whether they're buying it for their own use or for resale) and what commission is involved (i.e., what the agent will earn and what other people will earn). This applies if they are buying real estate for themselves or for any corporation or partnership in which they are shareholders, officers, or partners. If someone in the agent's family is interested in buying the property, it is a good idea for the agent to disclose the relationship.

Negotiating a Sale

When you, as a seller, receive an offer from a buyer, you have three choices. You can —

- accept everything exactly as written,
- reject the offer altogether, or
- counter the offer.

If you accept the offer as it is written, you have a legally binding contract to sell your home. If you reject the offer or make a counter-offer, you are entering into negotiation, because if you reject an offer, the buyer or the buyer's agent could ask you why you rejected it and make a new offer.

When you counter an offer, there is usually a time limit during which the counter-offer is valid. Once that time has expired, there is no offer in place. This is why it's important for a buyer to be available by phone, cell phone, or pager after he or she has made an offer. The buyer's agent must be able to contact the buyer with information of a seller's counter-offer. The same thing applies when the buyer counters your counter-offer. You should be around to receive it and respond to it.

Negotiating is a process that takes time, effort, understanding, and patience. For some people, this process is an art form that is perfected with experience. For others, negotiation is a stressful and difficult process, especially when it involves a real estate transaction. Many times, emotions take over. Lack of communication or jumping to conclusions can also lead to problems. For example, a seller may be insulted by a low-ball offer, when in fact the buyers have made an offer based on their financial capabilities as first-time home-buyers.

Face-to-face negotiations with a third party — either a real estate agent, lawyer, or other unbiased but knowledgeable person — are recommended to help you and the buyer achieve your goals. Remember that negotiation calls for compromise on both sides. Both parties have to listen and communicate effectively, and when it comes to real estate, this communication must be clearly set out in writing. Changes to the contract are not binding until they have been written down and initialed by both parties. Verbal offers and counter-offers can be rescinded at any time. (If there is so much crossing out and initialling on the contract that it becomes difficult to read, either party can draw up a new contract.

Make sure that it contains all the terms and conditions that you have agreed on.)

Promises or guarantees made by the seller outside the normal transaction, and outside the written contract of purchase and sale or agreement to purchase, must be written in an addendum that is signed and dated by both parties. Both the seller and the buyer should have a copy of the addendum so that there is no mistaking the legal responsibilities of both parties. If either the seller or buyer, or both, are using a lawyer or notary public, these people should also have copies of the addendum.

Sample 7 shows a contract of purchase and sale; Sample 8 shows an addendum. Look for them at the end of this chapter.

What to negotiate

Sellers often negotiate for a higher price than the buyer has offered, but there are other equally important items to negotiate, including the following:

- Condition precedents
- Condition precedents removal date
- Fixtures and chattels: Fixtures are items that stay with the property and are usually attached to it by a nail, screw, or something similar (i.e., light fixtures, wall-to-wall carpet). Chattels are not part of the property. Anything that is not for sale should be stated in your feature sheet and noted as an exclusion in the disclosure statement. A buyer may want to include items that you have excluded from the property for sale. You need to decide if you will agree to sell these and if you will negotiate to increase the sale price as a result.
- Closing and possession dates
- Down payment or deposit (After condition precedents have been removed, the deposit is usually increased to at least 5 percent of the sale price)

Selling your furniture

If you want to sell your furniture, this should be a separate entity and should not be included as part of the negotiations or purchase price. Deal with the contract of purchase and sale first, without any mention of the furniture, and afterwards let the buyers know that you are also interested in selling the furniture. Including this

The sale of a property is not final until all the condition precedents have been removed.

in the contract of purchase and sale could cause problems or complications with the offer.

Have a list that names each piece of furniture (include a digital photo so that there is no mistaking which coffee table you are referring to) and give this list to the buyers. If they are not interested in the furniture, this will not collapse the deal, as this issue was not included in the main body of the contract of purchase and sale.

When You Reach an Agreement

After you reach an agreement with a buyer, you still have to wait for all condition precedents to be removed before the sale is final. Many things can happen that could result in a sale not going through. For example, on the one hand, the buyer may not be able to get financing, the building inspection could reveal that major repairs are needed, or the buyer may feel there is not enough money in the contingency fund for a strata title property. If hiccups happen — as they sometimes do — seek legal counsel immediately and make sure that the buyer signs a release form or an addendum to indicate that he or she was unable to remove condition precedents.

On the other hand, you may suddenly change your mind about selling. Many sellers feel seller's remorse, especially when an offer and acceptance of an offer happen quickly, as they usually do. You may be able to rescind the offer while you are still negotiating simply by refusing to accept one of the buyer's changes, but you should talk to a lawyer first to obtain proper guidance in doing so. If both you and the buyer have signed the contract of purchase and sale, including all changes, and the condition precedents have been removed, you cannot back out of the contract unless you can prove you were not legally competent to enter into a contract.

Deposits and down payments

If you are selling your home on your own, it is important to remember that deposits for any real estate transaction should be made out in trust to a lawyer. It is important that the words "in trust" are written on the cheque so that there is no mistaking where the money will go.

In real estate transactions, only lawyers and real estate agencies are allowed to have trust accounts. The deposits should always be placed in trust immediately.

If one of the buyer's cheques comes back NSF ("not sufficient funds"), it is important that you let the buyer know immediately that this has happened. Perhaps it was due to a mistake at the bank — which may happen from time to time. If both the seller and the buyer are still interested in moving forward with the transaction, then both parties need to agree on a time limit by which a new bank draft or a certified cheque for the amount must be given to the seller. In order to avoid such a problem, sellers should only accept deposit monies in the form of a certified cheque or a bank draft to begin with.

If you negotiate an increase in the deposit, the contract should stipulate when, and at what amount, the deposit should be given to the seller or the seller's agent.

What if the building does not pass inspection?

There are three facets to a building inspection:

1. To cite problems that need to be addressed immediately.
2. To cite problems that will need to be addressed in the near future.
3. To provide maintenance programs.

If the building fails inspection — as may happen, especially if the seller did not do a pre-sale inspection — there are three likely scenarios:

1. The buyer walks away from his or her offer.
2. The buyer will renegotiate the price to reflect the amount of repairs that need to be done.
3. If the buyer agrees, the seller may do the repairs and not renegotiate the price. This may be tricky, as the buyer may want a guarantee of the work being done to a certain standard.

The art of negotiation comes into effect once again, as this is a volatile situation in which anything can happen. As a seller, you need to decide whether you would like the deal to collapse or if you want to renegotiate at this point. It is always a good idea to consult with the building inspector (even though his or her client is the buyer) or to see a copy of the report so that you can make a decision based on information from a qualified professional.

Showing after accepting an offer

Once you have accepted an offer, you should still show your property to potential buyers in case the first offer collapses. There are many things that need to happen, and the buyer needs to be satisfied, even after an offer is in place. It is always a good idea to show while there is still an interest in the property.

When Condition Precedents Are Met

After the conditions are removed, you need to make sure that the buyer has drawn up a new addendum that says the conditions have been removed and that the buyer and witnesses have signed this addendum. Also make sure anything that was changed or amended in the contract of purchase and sale is duly initialed or signed and is dated properly. All parties should have a copy of the contract to keep for their files.

Ensure that the down payment cheque has been deposited in trust at your lawyer's or real estate agent's office and that all pertinent documents have been sent to your conveyancer — the lawyer or notary who completes the transfer and register of title (the conveyancing) to the new owner.

Checklist 2 provides questions to ask yourself as you draw up a contract.

Checklist 2
THE CONTRACT

The following checklist will help remind you of the details to consider before you sign the contract:

❑ What offer was placed on your property? $_____

❑ Did you receive a counter-offer?

❑ If so, are you going to accept, reject, or make another counter-offer? (This process of counter-offers may continue until an agreement is reached.)

❑ Did you include a time and day in which your counter-offer will expire?

❑ Were legible copies of the contract provided to all parties?

❑ Were changes in the contract initialled by all parties?

❑ Were signatures obtained by all parties?

❑ Were signatures of witnesses obtained by all parties?

❑ When is the subject removal date? _____

❑ When is the inspection date? _____

❑ What down payment and/or deposit was made? $_____

❑ Is the deposit going to be paid in full or in stages? _____

❑ What is the completion date?_____

❑ What date does possession take place? _____

❑ Are there other dates you would like to negotiate? Specify: _____
_____

❑ Do you know what the price includes and doesn't include?

❑ Did the price include storage space? (If so, what number?_____)

❑ Did the price include parking stall(s)? (If so, what number(s)?_____)

Checklist 2 — Continued

❏ Are there items the buyer would like to negotiate that were not included in the purchase price (e.g., light fixtures, alarm system)? Specify: _____

_____

❏ Have all the subjects been removed from the contract? (For example, subject to a building inspection, financing, review of the property disclosure statement, by-laws, minutes, etc.)

❏ If attachments or schedules form part of the contract, are these referenced in the main contract?

❏ Is the contract drafted to your specifications and particular situation?

❏ Did you give a receipt to the buyer for the deposit and was it attached to the contract?

❏ If you have a realtor, is he or she keeping the lines of communication open between you and the buyer during the negotiations?

❏ Did you, as a seller, include your own subject conditions in the contract?

❏ Did you, as a seller, communicate these in writing as part of the contract?

❏ Now that an agreement has been reached, did you or your realtor make sure the contract has been initialled, signed, and duly witnessed to ensure it is a legally binding contract?

AGREEMENT OF PURCHASE AND SALE*

AGREEMENT OF PURCHASE AND SALE

Prepared by: _____   Date: _____
(Full legal name or agency)

Seller: _____   Buyer: _____

Seller: _____   Buyer: _____

Address: _____   Address: _____

_____   _____

Telephone: _____   Telephone: _____

❏ Resident of Canada

OR

❏ Non-Resident of Canada

Property

Address: _____

Municipality: _____   Postal Code: _____

Legal Description: _____   PID# _____

Purchase Price

The purchase price of the Property will be _____ dollars ($_____).

Deposit

A deposit of _____ dollars ($_____), which will form part of the purchase price, will be paid on the following terms:_____.

Terms and Conditions

The following terms and conditions for the purchase and sale of the property apply:

_____

Completion

The sale will be completed on_____ , 20 _____.

Possession

The Buyer will have vacant possession of the Property at 12:00 p.m. on_____ , 20 ____.

*Note: This is an example of an agreement of purchase and sale. Each province and territory may have different rules regarding the proper form to use. Check with a lawyer in your area in regards to the proper form to use.

Adjustments

The Buyer will assume and pay all taxes, rates, local improvement assessments, fuel, and utilities as of _____ , 20 ____ .

Included Items

The following items are also included in the Purchase Price:

_____

Excluded Items

The following items are excluded from the Purchase of the property:

_____

Offer

This offer, or counter-offer, will be open for acceptance until _____ o'clock _____

on _____ , 20 ____ and upon acceptance, there will be a binding Contract of Purchase and Sale on the terms and conditions set forth.

_____	_____	_____
Witness	Buyer	Print Name

_____	_____	_____
Witness	Buyer	Print Name

Acceptance

The Seller hereby accepts the above offer and agrees to complete the sale upon the terms and conditions set out in this agreement.

Seller's acceptance is dated _____ 20 _____ .

_____	_____	_____
Witness	Seller	Print Name

_____	_____	_____
Witness	Seller	Print Name

Sample 8
ADDENDUM

MLS No. _____ Date: _____

Re: Address: _____

Further to the contract of purchase and sale dated _____ made between

_____ as seller and _____ as buyer.

Subject to the following terms and conditions on or before the following date: _____

1. Obtaining financing.
2. Obtaining a title search.
3. Obtaining a copy of a disclosure statement regarding the property.
4. Building inspection.

Above conditions are for sole benefit of the buyer.

_____   _____
Buyer   Buyer

_____   _____
Witness   Witness

_____   _____
Seller   Seller

_____   _____
Witness   Witness

Chapter 10
CLOSING, COMPLETION, AND POSSESSION

buyer?

The completion date is the date on which the seller becomes the registered owner of the property. It occurs when the buyer pays the purchase price in trust to the seller's lawyer or notary. Closing is the process in which all the legal and financial obligations in your contract of purchase and sale will be met. Your agent, lawyer, or notary should keep you informed of the steps involved. The possession date is the day the buyers can move in.

The Closing Procedure

Once the condition precedents written in the contract of purchase and sale have been removed and you have a legally firm contract, the buyer will go through the "closing" procedure. He or she might retain a lawyer or notary to make the necessary inquiries regarding the property taxes, builder's liens, GST issues, commissions, deposit, and so on to determine the exact amount the buyer owes you on the completion date.

The lawyer will arrange an appointment at which the buyer can review and sign all the relevant documents. The documentation provides an overview of the total cost of this transaction (including adjustments — i.e., fees for utilities, property tax, insurance, etc.,

that the new owner owes for the balance of the year — the property transfer tax, and the lawyer or notary's legal fees and disbursements) and indicates how much money (if any) the buyer still owes to complete the purchase on the scheduled completion date. The buyer must make this balance of funds available to the lawyer or notary at least one business day before the completion date. Usually it is paid by way of a certified cheque or bank draft payable to the lawyer or notary in trust.

While this is happening, you need to make sure that everything is in order, especially with regards to your title to your property. If there is a lien on the property or a certificate of pending litigation, you will not be able to complete the sale. If you don't learn about an impediment until the completion date, and possession occurs on the very next day, there will be problems and the buyer may sue you for damages. An agent or lawyer should notice these issues well before closing and can deal with them in time. However, if you are a FSBO and have engaged a lawyer only to handle the transaction at the very last minute, it is up to you to be aware of any charges on your title.

If there are co-owners on the title, they must also sign the contract of purchase and sale in order for the sale to be legitimate. If the co-owners are out of the province or out of the country, you must have a power of attorney from them that allows you to act on their behalf. Talk to a lawyer about obtaining a valid power of attorney.

This is when you should make arrangements to move to a new home. Don't forget to make final utility payments at your old home, begin service at your next home, and fill out a change of address form at the post office. See Checklist 3 at the end of this chapter for a list of companies you should notify about your move.

What Happens at Completion?

On the completion date, your lawyer or notary will submit the transfer document (which transfers title to the property from you to the buyer) to the provincial land title office. Once the registration of the purchase is complete, and the funds are received from the buyer, you will meet with your lawyer or notary to finalize documents. He or she will give you a statement of adjustments (see Sample 9), which will spell out what you still owe on any of the following items:

- Property taxes
- Real estate agent's commission monies
- Lawyer's fees
- Fees to discharge your mortgage
- Outstanding fees to the strata corporation, including move-out fees
- Interest owing on any of these outstanding fees
- GST on services rendered

The notary or lawyer will ensure that if you owe monies to the bank, the agent, the property tax department, the property management company or strata corporation, or anyone else, they are paid before the net balance from the buyer is made available to you.

There may also be money owing to you in the form of credits for property tax or strata fees paid in advance.

Completion must be done on a weekday

Make sure that the completion date is not on a weekend or statutory holiday, as the land title office is closed during that time. If by some oversight the completion date does fall on a statutory holiday or a weekend, you should arrange to see your lawyer or notary at least a day or two before — when the land title office is open — so that there will not be any complications or delays.

If the completion day is on a holiday or weekend, and the buyer's lawyer is not able to register the buyer as the new owner of the property, then the seller can choose not to provide the keys until this has been done. Both parties will be irate and upset.

Further, it is always a good idea to make possession day a couple of days after completion day. This helps in the situation described above, when there is a delay in registering the new owner, and it is also a good idea because, as a seller, you want to make sure that the monies are transferred successfully and are in your account before you provide the buyers with the keys to your home. If there is any delay in obtaining paperwork, you don't want to be in a position where you have to decide whether or not to hand over the keys.

SELLER'S STATEMENT OF ADJUSTMENTS

VENDOR(S):

PURCHASER(S):

Civic: 3899 Main Street, Anycity, Anyprovince, Canada

Legal: Parcel Identifier 000-111-000-111, District Lot A

Completion Date: April 1, 20--

Adjustment Date: April 3, 20--

Possession Date: April 3, 20--

	Debit	Credit
Sale Price		$160,000.00
Purchaser's portion of annual utilities paid by Vendors. Utilities: $48.00 Credit Vendors April 3 to December 31, 2005 $48.00 X 273 ÷ 365		$35.90
Deposit 5% down payment	$8,000.00	
Balance vendor will receive	$152,035.90	
Totals	$160,035.90	$160,035.90

Hiccups at completion

Completion is not always a smooth transition from one owner to the next, and you should watch out for possible hiccups that may occur. For example, your buyer could have the same name as someone with a court judgment against him or her, and the bank may refuse to release funds, even though the buyer has signed an affidavit confirming that he or she is not the person named in the court judgment. You might discover that the garage or pool of the house that you are selling extends onto a neighbouring property, municipal setback, or utilities right-of-way, and you may be ordered to remove the encroaching structure. Or you could discover at the last minute that you owe money to the strata corporation for unpaid fines. A good lawyer or notary will be able to help you avoid these problems, or will assist in correcting them when they do occur and will expedite tasks that need to be done in order to clear title.

You may want to consult a lawyer or notary to avoid last-minute problems that could delay the sale.

Hiccups at completion may also mean delays at possession if the lawyer or notary was not able to get to the land title office on time to register transfer of ownership. If the buyer has purchased title insurance, however, the transaction can still close on time. Buyers can move in and take possession as scheduled, saving buyer and seller any additional costs and inconvenience.

Possession

The possession day is agreed to by both the buyer and the seller. It is important to note that possession typically occurs at 12:01 p.m. on the possession day and not a moment sooner. This means that you are legally responsible for anything that happens before that time. However, if you indicated a different time in the contract of purchase and sale, either later or earlier, then the time on the contract is what both parties should adhere to.

When do you hand over the keys?

It is important to provide keys to the buyer only at the exact time of possession — and only after you have received news from your lawyer or notary that the monies have been received and the title has been exchanged. There could be hiccups and delays, and you should make sure that you protect yourself, especially at the last minute!

Any fixtures you wish to exclude from the sale must be specified in writing.

Even if you are selling a rental property and you know that the tenants have already moved out, you should not provide the keys to the buyers any sooner than the possession day. The buyers may ask you to give them the keys earlier so they can repaint or make repairs, but you are still the registered owner of the property and, as such, are still liable should anything happen that causes damage or injury.

What should you leave behind on possession day?

On possession day, you should leave everything mentioned in the contract that is included in the purchase price. That means all fixtures should remain — things that are affixed to the walls, floors, or ceilings. That includes all window coverings, wall-to-wall carpets, light fixtures, and so on, unless they were specifically excluded in the contract of purchase and sale.

As a seller, you should leave everything that the buyers viewed — you cannot substitute any of the appliances, window coverings, or fixtures with replacements of a lesser value or quality. Buyers and buyers' agents are thorough and take photos for documentation to ensure that appliances are the same type, model, and colour as when they viewed them.

What should you **not** leave behind?

You should make sure that old, worn-out furniture, tattered area rugs, garbage, and anything else deemed part of the seller's chattels is completely removed from the premises. If the property has been rented to tenants, you should do a walk-through of the entire property to make sure that they have completely removed their belongings and have not taken anything that is not theirs to take away.

Though typically all fixtures are included in the purchase price of the home, you may have excluded certain specific items, either in a listing agreement with the real estate agent or in an addendum to the contract of purchase and sale. You should make sure these items are removed.

In addition, there may be fixtures, furniture, and chattels included in the purchase price that are not apparent to the buyer. For example, a storage locker and one or two parking spaces are often included in the purchase price of a strata title property. For a house, there may be a tool or garden shed, built-in vacuum cleaner, garburator, air-conditioner unit, or hot tub. A description of these should be included in the written contract or addendum. You should also stipulate whether the parking is rented, assigned, or titled.

Doing a walk-through with the buyer or buyer's agent

It is common practice for listing agents to walk through the property with their seller clients before releasing the keys to the buyer. This will ensure that everything is as it should be. Likewise, the buyer's agent will do a walk-through with the buyer to make sure that everything that was written in the contract has been left behind.

If you do not have an agent, you should walk through the property yourself with the buyers to make sure that they are satisfied. Some misunderstandings could still occur at this moment. Perhaps the buyers thought that the area rug was to be left behind, especially as it fit so nicely in the room. You will have to explain to them that it is considered a chattel and is not included in the purchase price. Another situation may be that former tenants may have left a locker full of items. Make sure, in the case of a condominium, that the parking spot and the storage lockers are empty.

A special touch

When you're leaving a home, it's always nice if you have taken the extra time to vacuum the rugs, remove the garbage, and leave the place as clean and tidy as possible. Provide keys, remote controls, and any pertinent information such as warranties and manuals for the new homeowners. Many sellers also leave a Welcome Home card and perhaps some flowers or freshly baked cookies for the new owners.

Checklist 3
SERVICE ARRANGEMENTS

Before the possession date, you need to inform the following service providers of the date you will be ending service at your old address and beginning service at your new home. Check the boxes that are applicable to your situation:

Place to notify	New address
Telephone company	❏
Post office	❏
School(s)	❏
Electricity/hydro	❏
Natural gas	❏
Cable/Internet provider	❏
Doctor	❏
Dentist	❏
Bank(s)	❏
Accountant	❏
Employer(s)	❏
Family Allowance	❏
CPP/QPP	❏
Old age security	❏
Insurance company:	
Vehicle	❏
Home	❏
Subscriptions:	
Newspaper	❏
Magazines	❏
Other_____	❏
Credit cards:	
_____	❏
_____	❏
_____	❏
Moving company	❏
Landlord, if renting	❏

CONCLUSION

If you decide to sell your home on your own, be aware that you are opening your home to strangers and that you could be placing yourself and your family in a vulnerable position. Don't forget that there are dishonourable people everywhere, so take all precautions to protect yourself and your property.

A lawyer or notary can help you avoid lawsuits, liabilities, and arbitrations, but you should learn as much as you can about real estate law. Errors in judgement — even if they are innocently made — or giving out misleading or inaccurate information could result in a lawsuit. Make sure that you take all the precautions necessary to avoid this by retaining the services of a lawyer or notary from the very beginning. Alternatively, you can list with a real estate agent and benefit from his or her experience while doing most of the work yourself.

Selling your home can be a rewarding and fulfilling experience when you take the time to educate yourself and do it right. Good luck!

Appendix 1
REAL ESTATE ASSOCIATIONS AND BOARDS

Canadian Real Estate Association (CREA)

If you would like to know more about a realtor's ethical obligations to you as a buyer or seller, CREA can provide this information. CREA can also help you outline the usual steps involved in buying a house through a realtor.

> 1600 – 344 Slater St.
> Ottawa, ON K1R 7Y3
> Telephone: (613) 237-7111
> Fax: (613) 234-2567
> Website: www.crea.ca

Saskatchewan Real Estate Commission

The Commission is responsible for licensing and disciplining real estate brokers in Saskatchewan, including investigating complaints.

> 231 Robin Cres.
> Saskatoon, SK S7L 6M8
> Telephone: (306) 374-5233
> Toll free: 1-877-700-5233
> Fax: (306) 373-5377
> Website: www.srec.sk.ca

Real Estate Council of Alberta

The Council regulates the real estate industry in Alberta. It investigates complaints against real estate agents and mortgage brokers.

340 – 2424 4th St. SW
Calgary, AB T2S 2T4
Telephone: (403) 228-2954
Toll free: 1-888-425-2754
Fax: (403) 228-3065
Website: www.reca.ca

Real Estate Council of British Columbia

900 – 750 West Pender St.
Vancouver, BC V6C 2T8
Telephone: (604) 683-9664
Toll free: 1-877-683-9664
Fax: (604) 683-9017
Website: www.recbc.ca

Provincial Associations and Boards

Alberta

The Alberta Real Estate Assoc.
310 – 2424 4th St. SW
Calgary, AB T2S 2T4
Telephone: (403) 228-6845
Toll free: 1-800-661-0231
Fax: (403) 228-4360
Website: www.abrea.ab.ca

Edmonton Real Estate Board Co-op.
14220 – 112th Ave.
Edmonton, AB T5M 2T8
Telephone: (780) 451-6666
Fax: (780) 452-1135
Website: www.ereb.com

Calgary Real Estate Board Co-op. Ltd.
300 Manning Road NE
Calgary, AB T2E 8K4
Telephone: (403) 263-0530
Fax: (403) 218-3688
Website: www.creb.com

British Columbia

British Columbia Real Estate Assoc.
600 – 2695 Granville St.
Vancouver, BC V6H 3H4
Telephone: (604) 683-7702
Fax: (604) 683-8601
Website: www.bcrea.bc.ca

Real Estate Board of Greater Vancouver
2433 Spruce St.
Vancouver, BC V6H 4C8
Telephone: (604) 730-3000
Fax: (604) 730-3101
Website: www.realtylink.org

Manitoba

Manitoba Real Estate Assoc.
1240 Portage Ave., 2nd Floor
Winnipeg, MB R3G 0T6
Telephone: (204) 772-0405
Toll free: 1-800-267-6019
Fax: (204) 775-3781
Website: www.realestatemanitoba.com

Winnipeg Real Estate Board
1240 Portage Ave.
Winnipeg, MB R3G 0T6
Telephone: (204) 786-8854
Fax: (204) 784-2343
Website: www.wreb.mb.ca

New Brunswick

New Brunswick Real Estate Assoc.
22 Durelle St., Unit 1
Fredericton, NB E3C 1N8
Telephone: (506) 459-8055
Fax: (506) 459-8057
Website: www.nbrea.ca

Saint John Real Estate Board Inc.
120 – 600 Main St.
Hilyard Place
Saint John, NB E2K 1J5
Telephone: (506) 634-8772
Fax: (506) 634-8775
Website: www0.mls.ca/boards/saintjohn/

Newfoundland

Newfoundland Real Estate Assoc.
28 Logy Bay Road
St. John's, NF A1A 1J4
Telephone: (709) 726-5110
Fax: (709) 726-4221
Website: www0.mls.ca/boards/newfoundland/

Nova Scotia

Nova Scotia Association of REALTORS®
100 – 7 Scarfe Court
Dartmouth, NS B3B 1W4
Telephone: (902) 468-2515
Toll free: 1-800-344-2001
Fax: (902) 468-2533
Website: www.nsar.ns.ca

Northwest Territories

Yellowknife Real Estate Board
201 – 5204 50th Ave., 2nd floor
Yellowknife, NT X1A 1E2
Telephone: (867) 920-4624
Fax: (867) 873-6387
Website: www0.mls.ca/boards/yellowknife/

Ontario

Ontario Real Estate Assoc.
99 Duncan Mill Rd.
Don Mills, ON M3B 1Z2
Telephone: (416) 445-9910
Fax: (416) 445-2644
Website: www.orea.com

Toronto Real Estate Board
1400 Don Mills Rd.
Don Mills, ON M3B 3N1
Telephone: (416) 443-8100
Fax: (416) 443-0797
Website: www.torontorealestateboard.com

Prince Edward Island

Prince Edward Island Real Estate Assoc.
75 St. Peter's Rd.
Charlottetown, PE CIA 5N7
Telephone: (902) 368-8451
Fax: (902) 894-9487
Website: www.peirea.com

Quebec

Fédération des Chambres Immobilières
   du Québec
600 chemin du Golf
Île des Soeurs, QC H3E 1A8
Telephone: (514) 762-0212
Fax: (514) 762-0365
Website: www.fciq.ca

Chambre immobilière du Grand Montréal
600 chemin du Golf
Île des Soeurs, QC H3E 1A8
Telephone: (514) 762-2440
Toll free in Quebec: 1-888-762-2440
Fax: (514) 762-1854
Website: www.cigm.qc.ca

Saskatchewan

Saskatchewan Real Estate Assoc.
231 Robin Cres.
Saskatoon, SK S7L 6M8
Telephone: (306) 373-3350
Toll free: 1-877-306-7732
Fax: (306) 373-5377
Website: www.saskatchewanrealestate.com

Association of Regina Realtors Inc.
1854 McIntyre St.
Regina, SK S4P 2P9
Telephone: (306) 791-2700
Fax: (306) 781-7940
Website: www.reginarealtors.com

Yukon

Yukon Real Estate Association
49 Waterfront Place
Whitehorse, YT Y1A 6V1
Telephone: (867) 633-4290
Fax: (867) 667-2299
Website: www.yrea.yk.ca

Appendix 2

RESOURCE LIST FOR OIL TANK SAFETY

Alberta

Petroleum Tank Management Association of Alberta (PTMAA)
980 – 10303 Jasper Ave.
Edmonton, AB T5J 3N6
Telephone: (780) 425-8265
Toll free: 1-866-222-8265
Fax: (780) 425-4722
Website: www.ptmaa.ab.ca

British Columbia

Office of the Fire Commissioner
PO Box 9490, Stn Prov Govt
Victoria, BC V8W 9N7
Telephone: (250) 387-2283
Fax: (250) 356-8508
Website: www.mcaws.gov.bc.ca/firecom/

Manitoba

Manitoba Labour and Immigration
Mechanical and Engineering Branch
200 – 401 York Ave.
Winnipeg, MB R3C 0P8

Telephone: (204) 945-3446
Fax: (204) 945-4556
Website: www.gov.mb.ca/labour/safety/mechanic.html

New Brunswick

New Brunswick Dept. of Environment and Local Government
PO Box 6000
Fredericton, NB E3B 5H1
Telephone: (506) 453-2690
Fax: (506) 457-4991
Website: www.gnb.ca/0009

Newfoundland

Canadian Oil Heat Association, Newfoundland Chapter
202 – 115 Apple Creek Blvd.
Markham, ON L3R 6C9
Telephone: (905) 946-0264
Fax: (905) 946-0316
Website: www.coha.ca

Nova Scotia

Nova Scotia Department of Environment and Labour
PO Box 697
5151 Terminal Road
Halifax, NS B3J 2T8
Telephone: (902) 424-5300
Fax: (902) 424-0503
Website: www.gov.ns.ca/enla/

Ontario

Technical Standards and Safety Authority (TSSA)
Centre Tower, 14th Floor
3300 Bloor St. West
Toronto, ON M8X 2X4
Telephone: (416) 734-3300
Toll free: 1-877-682-8772
Fax: (416) 231-1626
Website: www.tssa.org

Prince Edward Island

Department of Fisheries, Aquaculture, and Environment
PO Box 2000
Jones Building, 5th Floor
11 Kent St.
Charlottetown, PE C1A 7N8
Telephone: (902) 368-4880
Fax: (902) 368-4857
Website: www.gov.pe.ca

Québec

Environnement Québec/Ministry of the Environment
Édifice Marie-Guyart
675 boul. René-Lévesque Est
Québec, QC G1R 5V7
Telephone: (418) 521-3830
Toll free: 1-800-561-1616
Fax: (418) 646-5974
Website: www.menv.gouv.qc.ca

Saskatchewan

Saskatchewan Ministry of the Environment
3211 Albert St.
Regina, SK S4S 5W6
Telephone: (306) 953-3751
Toll free in Saskatechewan: 1-800-205-7070
Website: www.se.gov.sk.ca/

Environmental Resource Network inquiry line (within Saskatchewan only): 1-800-567-4224. Ask for the Hazardous Substances and Waste Dangerous Goods Regulations.

Yukon

Yukon Housing Corporation
410H Jarvis St.
Whitehorse, YT Y1A 2H5
Telephone: (867) 667-5759
Toll free in Yukon: 1-800-661-0408, local 5759
Fax: (867) 667-3664
Website: www.housing.yk.ca

Appendix 3
PROVINCIAL MINISTRIES AND DEPARTMENTS OF HOUSING

Alberta

Alberta Community Development
Standard Life Centre, 7th Floor
10405 Jasper Ave.
Edmonton, AB T5J 4R7
Telephone: (780) 422-0122
Fax: (780) 422-8462
Website: www.cd.gov.ab.ca

Alberta Seniors Housing Support Programs
PO Box 927
Edmonton, AB T5J 2L8
Telephone: (780) 422-0122
Toll free in Alberta: 1-800-310-0000
Fax: (780) 422-8462
Website: www.seniors.gov.ab.ca

British Columbia

Housing Policy Branch
PO Box 9952, Stn Prov Govt
Victoria, BC V8W 9N7
Telephone: (250) 387-7088

Fax: (604) 387-5120
Website: www.mcaws.gov.bc.ca/housing/

Manitoba

Residential Tenancies Branch
302 – 254 Edmonton St.
Winnipeg, MB R3C 3Y4
Telephone: (204) 945-2476
Fax: (204) 945-6273
Website: www.gov.mb.ca/finance/cca/rtb/

Newfoundland

Newfoundland and Labrador Housing Corporation
Department of Human Resources, Labour, and Employment
PO Box 220
2 Canada Drive
St. John's, NF A1C 5J2
Telephone: (709) 724-3000
Fax: (709) 724-3250
Website: www.nlhc.nf.ca/

New Brunswick

Department of Family and Community Services
PO Box 6000
Sartain MacDonald Building
551 King St.
Fredericton, NB E3B 1E7
Telephone: (506) 453-2001
Fax: (506) 453-7478
Website: www.gnb.ca/0017/Housing

Office of Chief Rentalsman
PO Box 6000
Fredericton, NB E3B 5H1
Telephone: (506) 453-2682
Fax: (506) 444-4494
Website: www.gnb.ca

Northwest Territories

Northwest Territories Housing Corporation
PO Box 2100
Yellowknife, NT X1A 2P6
Telephone: (867) 873-7898

Fax: (867) 669-7010
Website: www.nwthc.gov.nt.ca

Nova Scotia

Department of Community Services
PO Box 696
Halifax, NS B3J 2T7
Telephone: (902) 424-3280
Fax: (902) 424-0661
Website: www.gov.ns.ca/coms/hous/

Ontario

Ministry of Municipal Affairs and Housing
777 Bay St., 17th Floor
Toronto, ON M5G 2E5
Telephone: (416) 585-7000
Fax: (416) 585-6470
Website: www.mah.gov.on.ca/

Prince Edward Island

Residential Rental Property Division
Island Regulatory and Appeals Commission
PO Box 577
501 – 134 Kent St.
Charlottetown, PE C1A 7L1
Telephone: (902) 892-3501
Fax: (902) 566-4076
Website: www.irac.pe.ca/rental

Québec

Ministère des Affaires municipales, du Sport et du Loisir
10, rue Pierre-Olivier-Chauveau
Québec, QC G1R 4J3
Telephone: (418) 691-2019
Fax: (418) 644-4472
Website: www.mamsl.gouv.qc.ca

Société d'habitation du Québec
Direction des communications
1054, rue Louis-Alexandre-Taschereau
Aile Saint-Amable, 3e étage
Québec, QC G1R 5E7

Telephone: (418) 643-7676
Toll free: 1-800-463-4315
Fax: (418) 643-4560
Website: www.habitation.gouv.qc.ca

Saskatchewan

Community Resources and Employment
Housing Division
1855 Victoria Ave., 5th Floor
Regina, SK S4P 3V7
Telephone: (306) 787-4177
Toll free: 1-800-667-7567
Fax: (306) 787-1306
Website: www.dcre.gov.sk.ca/housing

Yukon

Yukon Housing Corporation
410H Jarvis St.
Whitehorse, YK Y1A 2H5
Telephone: (867) 667-5759
Toll free in Yukon: 1-800-661-0408, local 5759
Fax: (867) 667-3664
Website: www.housing.yk.ca

Appendix 4

CANADIAN ASSOCIATIONS OF HOME AND PROPERTY INSPECTORS

If you are seeking a home inspector, you can call your provincial listing below. The national listing provides general information. The national listing also provides a general checklist to ask during a short inspection of a home.

National Headquarters

64 Reddick Road
PO Box 507
Brighton, ON K0K 1H0
Telephone: (613) 475-5699
Toll free: 1-888-748-2244
Fax: (613) 475-1595
Website: www.cahpi.ca

Alberta

PO Box 27039
Tuscany RPO
Calgary, AB T3L 2Y1
Telephone: (403) 248-6893
Toll free: 1-800-351-9993
Fax: (403) 204-0898
Website: www.cahpi-alberta.com

Atlantic

3045 Robie St., #257
Halifax, NS B3K 4P6
Toll free: 1-888-748-2244
Website: www.cahpi-atl.com

British Columbia

PO Box 22010
Capri Centre PO
Kelowna, BC V1Y 9N9
Telephone: (250) 491-3979
Toll free: 1-800-610-5665
Fax: (250) 491-2285
Website: www.cahpi.bc.ca

Manitoba

287 Tache Ave.
PO Box 91
Winnipeg, MB R2H 3B8
Toll free: 1-888-748-2244
Website: www.cahi.mb.ca/main.htm

Ontario

PO Box 38108, Castlewood RPO
Toronto, ON M5N 3A8
Telephone: (416) 256-0960
Toll free: 1-888-744-6244
Fax: (905) 771-1079
Web site: www.oahi.com

Quebec

384 – 2539 boul. St-Charles
Kirkland, QC H9H 3C4
Telephone: (514) 234-2104
Fax: (514) 694-5895
Website: www.aibq.qc.ca

Saskatchewan

PO Box 26045
RPO Cornwall Centre
Regina, SK S4P 4J7
Toll free: 1-866-546-7888
Website: www.cahpi-sk.com

GLOSSARY

Addendum:

An addition to an offer in which changes made in the offer are noted.

Adjustments:

The money the seller receives back for utility fees, property taxes, insurance fees, etc. that he or she has already paid for the year.

Agreement to purchase:

See **contract of purchase and sale**.

Appraiser:

A person employed by a bank who will give an evaluation of what a home is worth based on land values, the home's condition, etc.

Assumable mortgage:

A mortgage that allows buyers to assume the mortgage from the seller instead of from a lending institution.

Back-up offer:

An offer that, once it has been accepted by the seller, sits in secondary position and waits until the first offer firms up or collapses.

Bridge financing:

A temporary loan that makes it possible for a seller to purchase a new home when that sale closes before the sale of his or her current home.

Building inspector:

An expert who thoroughly inspects buildings and provides a written report of defects that need to be addressed.

Buyer's agent:

The real estate professional who works on behalf of the buyer.

Canada Mortgage and Housing (CMHC) Market Analysis Centre:

A service provided by CMHC that assists buyers and sellers in understanding the current housing market.

Chattel:

An item that is not considered part of the property and that can be removed by the seller.

City assessment:

A municipality's assessment of the amount of property taxes payable to it for a specific property.

Closing:

The process after which all the legal and financial obligations in a contract of purchase and sale have been met.

Commission:

The fee a real estate agent receives for selling a house. It is usually stated as a percentage of the total sale price or as a fixed dollar amount.

Comparative market analysis (CMA):

A collection and analysis of market sales data for similar properties that have recently been sold. It assumes that the market value of a property is equal to the price recently paid for similar properties.

Competing offers:

Offers to purchase that have been made by two buyers at the same time.

Completion date:

The date on which a buyer becomes the registered owner of the property in exchange for paying the purchase price in trust to the seller's lawyer or notary.

Condition precedents:

Conditions that must be met in order for a contract to be fulfilled.

Condominium:

See **strata title ownership**.

Contingency fund:

A fund of money held in reserve by a strata corporation to pay for emergency repairs or other unforeseen events.

Contract of purchase and sale:

A statement of an agreement's terms and conditions, recorded in legal form.

Conveyancer:

The lawyer or notary who completes the transfer and register of title (the conveyancing) to the new owner

Co-operative:

A type of ownership in which buyers purchase shares in the company that owns a property; they become co-owners.

Co-ownership:

Ownership by more than one person.

Counter-offer:

An alternative offer made by either party in response to an offer.

Deposit:

An amount of money given with an offer to purchase to show that the offer is in earnest. It is usually about $100.

Detached home:

A home that stands alone without being attached to another building.

Down payment:

An initial partial payment made when a property is purchased.

Duplex:

A building containing two separate residences, either side by side or one on top of the other. (See also semi-detached.)

Empty nesters:

People whose children have left home or who have retired.

Exclusive listing:

An agreement in which a seller gives one agent or agency the authority to offer a property for sale, lease, or exchange during a specific time period. The seller agrees to pay the listing agent a commission, even if the seller eventually sells the property him or herself.

Fixed rate mortgage:

A mortgage contract that is written for terms ranging from 6 months to 10 years. Penalties may be triggered if the borrower wishes to end the contract before the term expires (early repayment).

Fixture:

An item in a building, or on land, that is considered part of the property; it is usually affixed to the property by a nail, screw, or something similar.

For sale by owner (FSBO):

A private sale between a seller and buyer, done without third parties (i.e., real estate agents) acting as intermediaries, or with an agent acting on behalf of the buyer only.

Form "B" or estoppel certificate:

A document that indicates how much money is in a strata corporation's contingency fund for emergencies.

Freehold:

Ownership of a property, with full use and control of the land and the buildings on it.

Genuine consent:

Knowledge that the buyers understand what they are buying and are aware of everything that could affect their title if they buy a property.

High-ratio loan:

A loan that allows the buyer to borrow more than 75 percent of the purchase price or the appraised value of the property, whichever is less.

Home stagers:

Companies that prepare homes for showing.

Investment property:

A property that the owner rents out to one or more tenants in order to make money.

Joint tenancy:

A type of ownership in which property is co-owned, common among those purchasing with a spouse or partner. If one party dies, the entire ownership automatically transfers to the survivor, without having to go through probate.

Leasehold:

Holding a property by lease for a defined period of time. The lessee owns the buildings and improvements but not the land.

Letter of commitment:

A letter from a lending institution stating how much it is willing to lend, at what rate, and on which terms.

Listing agent:

A real estate licensee hired by a seller to help sell property; an agency relationship is created in which the seller becomes the principal and the licensee becomes the agent of the seller.

Listing agreement:

A contract that sets out in writing the arrangement between a seller and a real estate agent.

Lock box:

A computerized system that provides the keys to an apartment building and unit for sale only to qualified agents who have obtained the box's security access code from the listing agent.

Low-ball offer:

An offer that is substantially lower than the price the seller is asking.

Maintenance fees:

Strata property fees that include the costs of insurance, management fees, and the upkeep of common property.

Manufactured home:

A factory-built residential structure, typically designed with wheels so that it can be moved from one place to another. It is often placed on a rented space called a "pad" in a manufactured home park. Also known as a mobile home or a pre-fab.

Market value:

The amount a home is worth in the current market, compared to other houses for sale or recently sold.

Mortgage:

An agreement to lend money to finance the purchase of property; the property is held as security for the loan.

Move-up buyer:

A buyer who is looking to move into a bigger or better home, such as a family with children moving from a two-bedroom home to a three- or four-bedroom home.

Multiple listing service (MLS):

A listing of properties for sale that is available to all real estate agents who are members of their local real estate board.

Multiple offers:

Offers made by more than two parties at the same time.

Notary:

A person who can perform certain legal duties, such as filing legal forms, but who is not a lawyer.

Open house:

An event in which a seller opens his or her house to real estate agents and the general public so that potential buyers can come in and look at it.

Open listing:

A relatively loose, verbal agreement in which the seller gives one or more real estate agencies the authority to find a buyer for a property.

Party wall:

The wall shared by two halves of a duplex or two units in a row house or apartment.

Portable mortgage:

A mortgage loan that can be transferred to another property when a person decides to move.

Possession date:

The date on which the buyer takes physical possession of a property.

Pre-qualification:

A buyer obtains approval from a bank that it will lend him a certain amount of money for a mortgage before the buyer places an offer on a home.

Pre-termination charges:

A penalty the borrower is charged by a lender if the borrower pays off a mortgage before the actual termination date.

Private sale:

See **for sale by owner**.

Property condition disclosure statement (PCDS):

A statement, signed by the seller, that provides a history and description of the condition of the property, including details of environmental, structural, and mechanical issues and water, sewage, plumbing, and renovation information. Also known as a disclosure statement.

Property taxes:

Taxes paid by the registered owner of a property to a municipality.

Real estate agent:

A person who assists in buying or selling real estate.

Replacement cost:

For an older house, the cost of replacing it with a modern equivalent.

Row housing:

See **townhouse**.

Semi-detached:

A housing unit that shares only one wall with an adjoining unit.

Stakeholder:

A stakeholder is like a deposit, but is usually less money. It can be as little as one dollar and is given with the offer to show intention.

Starter home:

A small home suitable for a young single or young couple.

Strata title ownership:

A type of housing ownership in which buyers not only own a unit, but share ownership of common areas such as hallways, garages, and elevators.

Subject clauses:

See **condition precedents**.

Survey certificate:

A certificate showing that a survey has been conducted to formally establish the boundaries of a property, to ensure that all buildings are within those boundaries, and to ensure that a house is not encroaching on other properties.

Tenancy in common:

A form of co-ownership in which each owner may or may not have the same amount of shares or rights. As a result, one party may sell his or her share without the permission of others.

Timeshare:

A property that is owned by several people who each have a right to use it for certain periods each year.

Title insurance:

A one-time premium that insures against defects in title that may otherwise prevent a transaction from closing or that may arise after the property is purchased.

Title search:

A search carried out to discover who is registered as the current owner of the property and if any registered mortgages, easements, restrictive covenants, or rights-of-way may affect the use or value of the property in a positive or negative way.

Townhouse:

One of a row of adjoined homes, usually all of a similar style.

Transfer document:

The document that transfers title to a property from the seller to the buyer.

Vendor take-back (VTB) mortgage:

A mortgage that allows home-buyers a chance to purchase a property with the help of the seller, who lends them a portion of the purchase price.

Zoning:

Local government specifications regarding the types of buildings that may be built on particular properties and how those buildings may be used; for example, as single- or multi-family residential units, as duplexes, or as commercial or industrial structures.